Our Home and (Native?) Land

Our Home and (Native?) Land

Darren Grimes

CONTENTS

INTRODUCTION

B rief History of Indigenous Peoples in Canada and Their Ancestral Lands

Before the arrival of European settlers, Indigenous peoples inhabited what is now known as Canada for thousands of years, living in harmony with the land. They were not mere inhabitants but stewards of the land, with complex societies, rich cultures, and deep spiritual connections to the territories they called home. These were not primitive peoples; they had sophisticated systems of governance, trade networks spanning vast distances, and an understanding of the environment that ensured sustainable living for generations.

Indigenous nations, such as the Haudenosaunee, Anishinaabe, Cree, Métis, Inuit, and many others, thrived across diverse landscapes—spanning from the Arctic tundra to the dense forests of the East, the vast plains of the West, and the rugged coasts of the Pacific. Each of these nations had their own languages, traditions, and ways of life, all intricately tied to the land they lived on.

This land was more than just a means of survival; it was a cornerstone of identity, spirituality, and community. The land provided food, shelter, and medicine, but it also held sacred sites, burial grounds, and places of immense cultural significance. The concept of land ownership, as understood by European settlers, was foreign to many Indigenous cultures. Instead, land was seen as a communal resource, something to be shared and respected, not owned or exploited.

For thousands of years, Indigenous peoples managed the land with a level of care and foresight that modern governments could only dream of emulating. They knew the cycles of nature, the migration patterns of animals, and the seasons of the plants. They practiced sustainable hunting, fishing, and agriculture long before the word "sustainability" became a buzzword in environmental circles. This was their land, their inheritance, passed down through generations with the understanding that it would be preserved for those yet to come.

But this harmonious existence was not to last. With the arrival of European settlers in the late 15th century, a dark chapter in the history of this land began. The Crown, under the guise of "discovery," embarked on a campaign of colonization that would forever alter the lives of Indigenous peoples. Lands that had been tended to and revered for millennia were suddenly declared terra nullius—nobody's land—by a Crown that saw itself as the ultimate authority. The irony, of course, is that the land was far from empty; it was teeming with life, both human and non-human, all of which was about to be disregarded in the face of European greed.

The Crown's claim to these lands was rooted in a sense of superiority, bolstered by a legal doctrine that viewed Indigenous peoples as inferior, if they were even considered at all. The Doctrine of Discovery, endorsed by European monarchs and the Church, granted Christian explorers the right to claim lands they "discovered" and assert dominion over the Indigenous peoples they encountered. This was not just an act of arrogance but a blatant act of theft, justified by the twisted logic of colonialism.

What followed was centuries of dispossession, betrayal, and violence. Treaties were signed, often under duress or through deception, promising Indigenous peoples protection and rights to their land. In reality, these treaties were systematically ignored or violated by the Crown, which saw them as mere formalities on the path to full control. The Royal Proclamation of 1763, often cited as a protective measure for Indigenous lands, was nothing more than a tool for the Crown to consolidate its power and control the westward expansion of settlers. It laid the groundwork for a system that would see Indigenous peoples gradually pushed off their lands, confined to reserves, and stripped of their rights and dignity.

The Crown and subsequent Canadian governments continued to erode Indigenous land rights through policies of assimilation, forced relocation, and cultural genocide. The Indian Act of 1876, one of the most oppressive pieces of legislation in Canadian history, codified this dispossession, stripping Indigenous peoples of their autonomy and placing their lands under the control of the federal government. Reserves were established—small, often infertile parcels of land where Indigenous peoples were expected to live out their days in poverty and isolation, their once vast territories now reduced to a fraction of their original size.

The history of Indigenous peoples in Canada is not just a story of survival but a story of resistance. Despite the relentless efforts of the Crown and the federal government to erase their cultures and steal their lands, Indigenous peoples have persisted. They have fought back through legal challenges, protests, and by maintaining their languages, traditions, and connections to the land. The resilience of Indigenous communities is a testament to their strength and a reminder that the land they have called home for millennia is not something that can be easily taken away.

As we reflect on this history, it is clear that the Crown's actions were not just an affront to Indigenous peoples but an assault on the very principles of justice and human dignity. The land that was taken—through violence, deceit, and coercion—was never theirs to give away in the first place. It belongs to the Indigenous peoples who have lived on it since time immemorial, and any attempt to reconcile this dark history must begin with the acknowledgment of this fundamental truth.

Introduction to the Concept of Land Dispossession and Its Impact on Indigenous Communities

Land dispossession—the forceful or deceitful removal of Indigenous peoples from their ancestral lands—stands as one of the most egregious acts of colonial violence perpetrated by the Crown and the subsequent Canadian governments. This systemic theft was not just about land; it was about power, control, and the deliberate dismantling of Indigenous cultures, economies, and ways of life. The impact of this dispossession has been profound, rippling through generations, leaving scars that are still visible today in the form of poverty, social dislocation, and the erosion of cultural practices.

At the heart of land dispossession lies a deep-seated arrogance and sense of entitlement, an inherent belief that the lands of what is now Canada were there for the taking by European settlers. The Crown, with its imperial ambitions, viewed these lands as vast, untapped resources waiting to be exploited for the benefit of the empire. This mindset completely disregarded the fact that these lands were already home to diverse and thriving Indigenous nations, each with its own systems of governance, stewardship, and cultural significance attached to the land.

The dispossession of Indigenous lands was not a series of isolated incidents but a calculated and coordinated effort by the Crown and its colonial administrators to cement their control over the continent. This process began with the early treaties, which were often signed under duress or without a full understanding by Indigenous leaders of the implications. These treaties, touted by the Crown as agreements of peace and mutual benefit, were in reality instruments of control, used to gradually chip away at Indigenous land holdings while making grand promises that were rarely, if ever, kept.

The introduction of the reserve system further entrenched this dispossession. By confining Indigenous peoples to small, often inhospitable parcels of land, the Crown effectively severed their connections to the vast territories that had sustained them for generations. The land reserved for Indigenous communities was a mere fraction of what they had once freely inhabited and was often land that the settlers and the Crown deemed undesirable for agricultural or economic development.

This was no accident; it was a deliberate tactic to weaken Indigenous societies by stripping them of their most valuable resource—their land.

The Indian Act of 1876 was perhaps the most blatant legal tool of dispossession. It not only formalized the reserve system but also placed all aspects of Indigenous life, including land use, under the strict control of the federal government. Indigenous peoples were no longer seen as autonomous nations with inherent rights to their lands but as wards of the state, subject to the whims and policies of a government that had little regard for their well-being. This act institutionalized the theft of Indigenous lands, making it nearly impossible for communities to reclaim what was taken from them.

The impact of land dispossession on Indigenous communities cannot be overstated. Economically, it has left many Indigenous peoples trapped in a cycle of poverty, with limited access to the natural resources that once provided their livelihoods. Traditional hunting, fishing, and farming practices have been disrupted, leading to food insecurity and dependence on government assistance. The loss of land has also meant the loss of economic opportunities that come with it, such as the ability to develop land for agriculture, industry, or tourism.

Culturally, the effects have been equally devastating. Land is not just a physical space but a repository of cultural knowledge, practices, and spiritual beliefs. The forced removal from traditional territories has severed the ties that bind Indigenous peoples to their ancestors and their cultural heritage. Sacred sites have been desecrated, traditional languages and practices have been marginalized, and the cultural continuity that is so vital to the identity of Indigenous communities has been severely disrupted.

Socially, the displacement and dispossession of land have contributed to a host of issues, including the fragmentation of communities, loss of social cohesion, and the erosion of traditional governance structures. The reserve system, with its rigid boundaries and isolation from broader society, has fostered a sense of alienation and disconnection among Indigenous peoples. The imposition of foreign governance systems, coupled with the loss of land, has undermined the authority of traditional leaders and disrupted the social fabric of Indigenous communities.

The psychological impact of land dispossession is another critical aspect that is often overlooked. The trauma of losing one's homeland, of being forcibly removed or coerced into giving up land, has left deep emotional scars. This trauma has been passed down through generations, manifesting in various forms of social and mental health issues, including depression, substance abuse, and a sense of hopelessness. The disconnection from the land, which is so central to Indigenous identity and well-being, has had profound effects on the mental and emotional health of Indigenous peoples.

Moreover, the dispossession of land has also had political consequences. It has weakened the ability of Indigenous nations to assert their sovereignty and self-determination. Without control over their land, Indigenous peoples have been marginalized in the political processes that affect their lives. The struggle to regain land rights and to assert control over natural resources has been long and arduous, often met with resistance from a government that is more interested in maintaining its own power and control than in addressing historical injustices.

Despite these immense challenges, Indigenous communities have not remained silent in the face of dispossession. Over the years, they have mobilized, resisted, and fought back, using every tool at their disposal—legal battles, protests, and international advocacy—to reclaim their lands and assert their rights. The resurgence of land claims and the growing recognition of Indigenous rights in recent decades are a testament to the resilience and determination of Indigenous peoples to reclaim what was taken from them.

In conclusion, land dispossession is not just a historical injustice; it is an ongoing reality that continues to shape the lives of Indigenous peoples in Canada. The Crown and the Canadian government have a long and sordid history of exploiting Indigenous lands for their own gain, with little regard for the consequences on the communities they dis-placed. The impact of this dispossession is far-reaching, affecting every aspect of Indigenous life, from the economy to culture, social struc-tures, and mental health. As we move forward, it is imperative that we address these injustices head-on, acknowledging the truth of what hap-pened and working towards a future where Indigenous peoples have control over their lands and destinies. The fight for land rights is not just a struggle for territory; it is a fight for justice, dignity, and the survival of Indigenous cultures and communities.

The Importance of Land Rights in the Context of Cultural Preser-vation, Autonomy, and Economic Development

The question of land rights is not merely a legal or territorial issue; it is a matter that strikes at the very heart of Indigenous identity, culture, and survival. For Indigenous peoples in Canada, land is not just a re-source to be exploited; it is a living entity that sustains their way of life, their spirituality, and their connection to past and future generations. The importance of land rights in this context cannot be overstated, as they are crucial for the preservation of culture, the assertion of auton-omy, and the pursuit of economic development that aligns with Indige-nous values and aspirations.

Cultural Preservation

Land is the foundation of Indigenous cultures. It is where cere-monies are held, where ancestors are honored, and where traditional knowledge is passed down through generations. The land is imbued with stories, teachings, and spiritual significance that form the core of Indigenous identity. When Indigenous peoples are disconnected from their lands, they are not just losing physical space; they are being severed from their cultural roots.

The forced relocation of Indigenous peoples to reserves and the sub-sequent erosion of their traditional territories have had devastating ef-fects on cultural preservation. Sacred sites have been desecrated or lost to development, traditional languages have been marginalized, and cultural practices have been disrupted. Without access to their ancestral lands, Indigenous peoples are unable to fully practice their cultures, which are inherently tied to specific landscapes and ecosystems.

Land rights are therefore essential for the preservation and revitalization of Indigenous cultures. When Indigenous communities regain control over their lands, they are able to protect sacred sites, maintain traditional land-based practices, and pass on cultural knowledge to future generations. This is not just about preserving the past; it is about ensuring that Indigenous cultures continue to thrive and evolve in the face of ongoing challenges.

The recognition of land rights also serves as a powerful tool for cultural affirmation. It acknowledges the deep connection between Indigenous peoples and their lands and affirms their right to maintain and strengthen that connection. This recognition is a critical step towards healing the wounds of colonialism and rebuilding the cultural foundations that have been eroded by centuries of dispossession.

Autonomy and Self-Determination

Land rights are inextricably linked to the concept of autonomy and self-determination. For Indigenous peoples, the ability to control and manage their own lands is a fundamental aspect of their sovereignty and nationhood. Without land, there can be no true self-determination, as the land is the basis upon which communities build their political, social, and economic systems.

The colonial imposition of the reserve system and the continued control of Indigenous lands by the federal government through the Indian Act have severely undermined Indigenous autonomy. These policies have reduced Indigenous peoples to mere tenants on their own lands, subject to the whims and regulations of a government that has historically acted in its own interests rather than those of Indigenous communities.

Asserting land rights is a critical step in reclaiming autonomy and self-governance. When Indigenous peoples have control over their lands, they can make decisions that reflect their values, priorities, and ways of life. This includes decisions about resource management, environmental stewardship, and community development. Land rights enable Indigenous nations to govern themselves according to their own laws and traditions, free from external interference.

The importance of land rights in this context is also evident in the growing movement towards Indigenous-led governance and the creation of self-governing agreements. These agreements, which often include land settlements, represent a shift towards recognizing Indigenous sovereignty and the right to determine their own futures. They provide a framework for Indigenous nations to exercise their authority over their lands and resources, in line with their own cultural values and priorities.

Economic Development

Land is not just a cultural and spiritual asset; it is also a critical economic resource. For Indigenous communities, the ability to develop and manage their lands is essential for achieving economic self-sufficiency and prosperity. However, the legacy of land dispossession has left many Indigenous peoples without the means to fully participate in the economy, trapping them in a cycle of poverty and dependence on government assistance.

The reserve system, which confines Indigenous peoples to small and often economically unviable parcels of land, has severely limited their ability to engage in economic activities. Reserves are often located in remote areas, far from markets and infrastructure, making it difficult to develop businesses, access jobs, or generate income. Furthermore, the restrictions imposed by the Indian Act, which limits the ability of Indigenous peoples to fully own or leverage their land, have stifled economic development on reserves.

Land rights are therefore crucial for unlocking the economic potential of Indigenous communities. When Indigenous peoples have control over their lands, they can pursue economic development on their own terms. This includes opportunities in agriculture, tourism, resource extraction, and other sectors that align with their cultural and environmental values. By reclaiming their lands, Indigenous communities can create jobs, generate income, and build the infrastructure needed to support long-term economic growth.

Moreover, the assertion of land rights often comes with the potential for revenue sharing and benefit agreements with governments and corporations. These agreements can provide Indigenous communities with a share of the profits from resource development on their lands, helping to build economic resilience and reduce dependence on external funding. However, it is crucial that these agreements are negotiated in a way that respects Indigenous sovereignty and ensures that the benefits are distributed equitably within the community.

Land rights also open up opportunities for partnerships and collaborations that can drive economic development. Indigenous communities that have secured their land rights are better positioned to negotiate with governments, businesses, and investors on equal footing. This can lead to the development of projects that create sustainable economic opportunities while preserving the environmental and cultural integrity of the land.

Conclusion

The importance of land rights for Indigenous peoples in Canada cannot be overstated. Land is the foundation of Indigenous cultures, the basis of their autonomy, and the key to their economic development. Without land, Indigenous peoples are deprived of the ability to fully express their identities, govern themselves, and build prosperous futures for their communities.

The ongoing struggle for land rights is not just a fight for territory; it is a fight for justice, dignity, and the right to determine one's own destiny. It is a fight against the legacy of colonialism that has sought to erase Indigenous peoples from their lands and histories. By reclaiming their land rights, Indigenous communities are not only asserting their sovereignty but also laying the groundwork for a future where they can thrive as distinct and self-determined nations.

As Canada grapples with the legacy of its colonial past, it is imperative that land rights are recognized and respected as a fundamental human right. The path to reconciliation must include the restitution of land and the recognition of Indigenous peoples' inherent rights to their territories. Only then can we begin to address the deep injustices that have been inflicted upon Indigenous communities and move towards a future of true justice, equality, and respect for all.

Purpose of the Book

The purpose of this book is to shed light on one of the most enduring and egregious injustices in Canadian history: the dispossession of Indigenous lands. Through a detailed examination of the historical and ongoing processes that have stripped Indigenous peoples of their territories, this book seeks to provide a comprehensive understanding of the deep-rooted issues that continue to shape the relationship between Indigenous communities and the Canadian state. This is not just a recounting of past wrongs; it is a call to action, a demand for justice, and a roadmap for reclaiming what has been stolen.

Exploring the Historical and Ongoing Processes of Land Dispossession in Canada

At the heart of Canada's creation as a nation lies a dark and often overlooked truth: the systematic and calculated theft of Indigenous lands. From the first days of European colonization, the Crown and its agents embarked on a relentless campaign to seize control of the vast territories that Indigenous peoples had inhabited, cared for, and thrived upon for millennia. This book will explore how this process unfolded—through deceitful treaties, the imposition of the reserve system, and the legislative straitjacket of the Indian Act.

But this is not merely a history lesson. The processes of land dispossession are not relics of the past; they continue to this day, albeit in more subtle and insidious forms. Land claims that drag on for decades, government policies that prioritize corporate interests over Indigenous rights, and the ongoing refusal to honor treaties are all part of the modern-day continuation of this colonial legacy. This book will delve into these contemporary issues, exposing how the same mechanisms of control and exploitation that were used centuries ago are still at play today.

The goal is to provide readers with a clear and unflinching view of how land dispossession has shaped the lives of Indigenous peoples across Canada. By understanding the full scope of this injustice, we can begin to grasp the profound impact it has had on Indigenous communities—culturally, economically, and politically. This exploration is crucial for anyone who seeks to understand the true history of Canada and the ongoing struggles for justice that define this country's relationship with its Indigenous peoples.

Analyzing the Legal, Political, and Social Struggles for Indigenous Land Rights

The struggle for Indigenous land rights in Canada is a battle fought on multiple fronts—legal, political, and social. It is a struggle against a colonial system that has consistently placed the interests of settlers and the state above those of the Indigenous nations whose lands were stolen. This book will analyze these struggles in depth, examining the legal battles that have been waged in courts, the political movements that have risen to challenge the status quo, and the social activism that has galvanized communities across the country.

On the legal front, this book will explore landmark cases such as the Calder case, which first recognized Aboriginal title in Canadian law, and the more recent Tsilhqot'in Nation decision, which granted a First Nation title to a specific area of land. These cases are significant not only for their outcomes but for what they reveal about the legal system's slow and often begrudging recognition of Indigenous rights. The legal analysis will also cover the limitations and challenges faced by Indigenous communities in seeking justice through a system that was designed to uphold colonial interests.

Politically, the struggle for land rights is intertwined with the broader fight for Indigenous sovereignty and self-determination. This book will examine the role of Indigenous political organizations, such as the Assembly of First Nations, in advocating for land rights and how these efforts have been met with resistance and co-optation by federal and provincial governments. The analysis will also consider the role of non-

Indigenous allies and the importance of solidarity in advancing the cause of land rights.

Socially, the book will highlight the grassroots movements that have been instrumental in bringing attention to land rights issues. From the Idle No More movement to the blockades and protests that have arisen in response to pipeline projects and resource extraction on Indigenous lands, these acts of resistance are a testament to the resilience and determination of Indigenous peoples to protect their lands and assert their rights. The book will explore how these movements have shifted public consciousness and forced a reckoning with the colonial foundations of Canada.

Through this analysis, the book aims to demonstrate that the struggle for Indigenous land rights is not just a legal or political issue; it is a fundamental question of justice and human rights. The persistence of these struggles highlights the ongoing failure of the Canadian state to fully recognize and respect the inherent rights of Indigenous peoples. By bringing these issues to the forefront, this book seeks to contribute to the broader conversation about how we can move towards a more just and equitable future.

Proposing Pathways Toward a More Equitable Future for Indigenous Land Ownership and Control

This book is not just about documenting past and present injustices; it is about envisioning and advocating for a future where Indigenous land rights are fully recognized, respected, and restored. The final part of this book will propose pathways towards a more equitable future for Indigenous land ownership and control, offering concrete recommendations for change.

One of the central arguments of this book is that true reconciliation cannot occur without the restitution of land. This means not only recognizing Indigenous title to land but also returning significant portions of land to Indigenous control. The book will explore various models for land restitution, including the use of land trusts, co-management agreements, and the creation of new frameworks for land governance that prioritize Indigenous sovereignty.

In addition to restitution, the book will argue for the need to overhaul the legal and political systems that have perpetuated land dispossession. This includes the repeal or significant reform of the Indian Act, the implementation of the United Nations Declaration on the Rights of Indigenous Peoples (UNDRIP) in a way that goes beyond mere symbolism, and the establishment of mechanisms for meaningful consultation and consent in all decisions affecting Indigenous lands.

The book will also address the economic dimensions of land rights, proposing ways in which Indigenous communities can build sustainable economies that are rooted in their land and cultural practices. This includes exploring opportunities for economic development that align with Indigenous values, such as eco-tourism, renewable energy projects, and the sustainable management of natural resources. The goal is to envision a future where Indigenous communities are not only the stewards of their lands but also the primary beneficiaries of the wealth those lands generate.

Finally, the book will call for a broader societal shift in how land is understood and valued in Canada. It will argue that non-Indigenous Canadians have a role to play in supporting Indigenous land rights, whether through advocacy, education, or the relinquishing of lands currently held by settlers. This is about more than just legal rights; it is about acknowledging the moral and ethical responsibility to address the wrongs of the past and build a future based on justice, respect, and mutual recognition.

In conclusion, the purpose of this book is to challenge the status quo, to demand accountability from those in power, and to offer a vision for a future where Indigenous land rights are fully realized. It is a call to action for all those who believe in justice, equity, and the fundamental right of Indigenous peoples to reclaim their lands and their futures.

Chapter 1: The Pre-Colonial Era

Indigenous Land Stewardship and Territorial Control

Long before the arrival of European settlers, Indigenous peoples across what is now Canada practiced a sophisticated and deeply ingrained system of land stewardship and territorial control. This stewardship was not merely a means of survival but a way of life, deeply intertwined with spiritual, cultural, and social practices. Indigenous land stewardship was characterized by a profound respect for the natural world, a recognition of the interconnectedness of all life, and a commitment to ensuring the sustainability of resources for future generations. The arrival of European colonizers, however, brought with it an entirely different approach to land—one rooted in exploitation, ownership, and domination. The clash between these two worldviews would set the stage for centuries of conflict, dispossession, and resistance.

A Philosophy of Stewardship

For Indigenous peoples, the land was not just a resource to be exploited but a living entity that was to be cared for and respected. This stewardship was guided by a philosophy that emphasized balance, reciprocity, and responsibility. The land provided everything that was needed—food, medicine, shelter, and spiritual sustenance—but it also required care in return. This relationship was maintained through a deep understanding of the environment, accumulated over thousands of years of living in harmony with the natural world.

Indigenous stewardship practices were diverse, reflecting the varied ecosystems across the continent. In the forests of the Pacific Northwest, Indigenous peoples managed vast tracts of land through controlled burns, which promoted the growth of key resources like berries and game animals. In the plains, the buffalo was central to the way of life, and Indigenous peoples carefully managed hunting practices to ensure the herds remained robust. Along the coasts, sustainable fishing practices were developed, including the construction of fish weirs and the careful management of shellfish beds.

These practices were not haphazard or primitive; they were the result of careful observation, experimentation, and a deep understanding of ecological processes. Indigenous peoples knew when to harvest certain plants and animals, how to rotate hunting and gathering areas to prevent depletion, and how to manage the land in a way that ensured its long-term health and productivity. This knowledge was passed down through generations, often encoded in stories, ceremonies, and cultural practices that reinforced the importance of respecting the land and its resources.

Territorial Control and Governance

Indigenous territorial control was equally complex and varied. Territories were often clearly defined and recognized by neighboring groups, with boundaries marked by natural features such as rivers, mountains, or specific landmarks. These territories were governed by Indigenous laws and customs, which dictated how land could be used, who had access to it, and how conflicts over land were to be resolved.

Unlike the European concept of land ownership, which is rooted in individual rights and the commodification of land, Indigenous territorial control was based on collective responsibility and communal use. The land was held in trust by the community, with specific areas designated for hunting, fishing, gathering, and other activities that supported the group's well-being. Decisions about land use were often made collectively, with leaders consulting with elders, knowledge keepers, and other community members to ensure that the needs of all were met while maintaining the health of the land.

Indigenous governance systems were highly sophisticated, with many nations having formal councils, leaders, and decision-making processes. These systems were not static but adapted to changing circumstances, such as shifts in population, environmental changes, or new relationships with other groups. Treaties and alliances were often used to establish peace and mutual respect between neighboring nations, with land use and access being key components of these agreements.

The concept of land as a shared resource was central to these governance systems. Access to land and resources was often based on relationships rather than ownership, with individuals and families having specific rights and responsibilities within the broader community. This approach ensured that the land was used sustainably and that its benefits were distributed fairly among all members of the community.

The Disruption of Colonialism

The arrival of European colonizers disrupted these systems of stewardship and territorial control in profound and devastating ways. The imposition of European notions of land ownership, based on the Doctrine of Discovery and terra nullius, fundamentally clashed with Indigenous understandings of land and territory. To the colonizers, the land was empty—free for the taking—and Indigenous peoples were seen as obstacles to be removed or assimilated.

Colonial policies, such as the creation of reserves and the implementation of the Indian Act, systematically dismantled Indigenous systems of land stewardship and governance. Indigenous peoples were forcibly removed from their territories, confined to small, often unproductive parcels of land, and stripped of their ability to manage the land according to their traditional practices. The imposition of European legal systems, which recognized only the Crown's authority over land, further eroded Indigenous control and reduced them to tenants on their own lands.

The environmental degradation that followed colonial expansion was a direct result of this disruption. The overexploitation of resources, the destruction of ecosystems, and the disregard for the long-term health of the land were all hallmarks of the colonial approach to land. In contrast to the sustainable practices of Indigenous peoples, the colonizers viewed the land as a commodity to be exploited for immediate gain, with little regard for the consequences.

The Resurgence of Indigenous Stewardship

Despite the immense challenges posed by colonialism, Indigenous peoples have never relinquished their connection to the land or their commitment to stewardship. Across Canada, there is a growing resurgence of Indigenous land stewardship, driven by a desire to reclaim traditional practices, restore ecosystems, and assert sovereignty over Indigenous territories.

Indigenous-led conservation initiatives, such as the establishment of Indigenous Protected and Conserved Areas (IPCAs), are redefining how land and resources are managed. These initiatives are based on the principles of Indigenous knowledge and governance, offering an alternative to the top-down, extractive approaches that have dominated land management in Canada. By asserting their rights to manage their lands, Indigenous communities are not only protecting the environment but also revitalizing their cultures and strengthening their economies.

Legal victories, such as the recognition of Aboriginal title in the Tsilhqot'in Nation case, have also opened the door for Indigenous peoples to reclaim control over their territories. These victories, while hard-fought and often limited in scope, represent important steps toward the restoration of Indigenous land rights and the recognition of Indigenous sovereignty.

In conclusion, Indigenous land stewardship and territorial control are foundational to the identities, cultures, and survival of Indigenous peoples in Canada. The disruption caused by colonialism has had devastating effects, but the resurgence of Indigenous stewardship offers hope for a future where Indigenous peoples can once again manage their lands according to their own laws and traditions. This book will explore these themes in depth, shedding light on the importance of land rights in the broader struggle for justice, sovereignty, and cultural survival. The path forward is clear: it begins with the recognition of Indigenous land rights and the return of control over these lands to the people who have cared for them since time immemorial.

Traditional Land Use Practices and the Deep Connection Between Indigenous Peoples and Their Territories

For Indigenous peoples in Canada, the land is not merely a place to inhabit; it is a vital, living entity intertwined with their cultural, spiritual, and social identities. The connection to the land is profound, rooted in thousands of years of careful stewardship and sustainable use. Traditional land use practices are the embodiment of this relationship, reflecting a deep understanding of the environment and a commitment to maintaining the balance between human needs and the health of the land.

Traditional Land Use Practices

Indigenous land use practices were shaped by a deep respect for the natural world and a recognition of the interconnectedness of all life forms. These practices were not imposed upon the land but emerged from a reciprocal relationship, where the land provided for the people, and in return, the people cared for the land. This reciprocal relationship was central to Indigenous worldviews and underpinned the sustainability of their societies.

Hunting and Gathering:

Hunting and gathering were central to the livelihoods of many Indigenous peoples, particularly in regions where agriculture was less viable. Indigenous hunters, such as the Cree and the Dene, developed extensive knowledge of animal behavior, migration patterns, and the ecology of their territories. They practiced selective hunting, targeting specific animals at the right time of year to ensure the sustainability of populations. For example, the Plains Cree had strict rules about when and how bison could be hunted, ensuring that herds remained healthy and plentiful.

Gathering was similarly governed by careful observation and respect for the natural cycles. Indigenous women, who were often responsible for gathering, knew when and where to collect plants, berries, and medicinal herbs without depleting these resources. They practiced rotational harvesting, allowing areas to regenerate before returning to them, thus maintaining the land's productivity over time.

Agriculture:

In regions like the Great Lakes and St. Lawrence River valleys, Indigenous peoples such as the Haudenosaunee (Iroquois) practiced agriculture, cultivating crops like corn, beans, and squash—known as the "Three Sisters." These crops were grown together in a symbiotic relationship that enriched the soil and provided a balanced diet. The Haudenosaunee used techniques such as crop rotation and the intercropping of plants to maintain soil fertility and prevent erosion.

Agriculture was not just a means of food production; it was a spiritual practice deeply connected to the cycles of the seasons and the land. Ceremonies were held to honor the spirits of the plants and ensure successful harvests. The relationship with the land was one of gratitude and stewardship, with an understanding that the earth's bounty was a gift that required care and respect.

Fishing:

Indigenous peoples along the coasts and inland waterways, such as the Haida, Mi'kmaq, and Anishinaabe, developed sophisticated fishing techniques that sustained their communities for generations. These included the use of fish weirs, traps, and nets that allowed for the selective harvesting of fish while ensuring that breeding populations remained strong.

Indigenous fishing practices were guided by knowledge of fish behavior and an understanding of the aquatic ecosystems. For example, the Mi'kmaq people managed eel fisheries through the use of weirs and seasonal restrictions, allowing eel populations to remain healthy and abundant. These practices ensured that fishing could continue year after year without depleting the resource.

Fire Management:

Fire was an essential tool for many Indigenous peoples, particularly in the boreal forests and grasslands. Controlled burns, also known as "cultural burning," were used to manage the landscape, clear underbrush, promote the growth of certain plants, and maintain open areas for hunting. The Anishinaabe and other Indigenous nations in what is now Ontario and Manitoba used fire to enhance the growth of blueberries and to maintain the open prairie landscapes that supported diverse plant and animal species.

These burns were conducted with a deep understanding of the local ecology and were timed to coincide with specific seasons and weather conditions. The use of fire not only improved hunting and gathering opportunities but also reduced the risk of catastrophic wildfires by removing excess fuel from the forest floor.

Spiritual and Cultural Practices:

Indigenous land use practices were deeply embedded in spiritual and cultural traditions. The land was seen as sacred, and its resources were gifts from the Creator. Ceremonies, such as the potlatch of the Pacific Northwest Coast peoples or the Sun Dance of the Plains Nations, were often tied to the land and its cycles, reinforcing the connection between the people and their territories.

Sacred sites, such as mountains, rivers, and specific land formations, were integral to Indigenous spiritual practices. These sites were often places of pilgrimage, healing, and ceremony, and they were carefully protected and maintained by the community. The respect for these sacred spaces was passed down through generations, ensuring that the spiritual connection to the land remained strong.

Deep Connection to the Land

The connection between Indigenous peoples and their territories is not just a matter of practicality; it is a fundamental aspect of their identity and way of life. The land is more than just a physical space; it is a living entity that holds the history, stories, and spirits of the people who inhabit it. This connection is expressed through language, oral traditions, and cultural practices that emphasize the importance of maintaining a harmonious relationship with the land.

Identity and Belonging:

The land is integral to the identity of Indigenous peoples. It is the source of their language, culture, and traditions. The names of places, plants, animals, and natural features are often embedded in Indigenous languages, reflecting a deep understanding of the environment. These names carry stories and knowledge that have been passed down through generations, connecting the people to their ancestors and to the land itself.

Belonging to a specific territory is a source of pride and identity for Indigenous communities. The land is where their ancestors lived, where their cultural practices were developed, and where their future generations will continue to thrive. This sense of belonging is reinforced through land-based education, where children learn about their environment, culture, and history by spending time on the land.

Spiritual Connection:

The land is sacred to Indigenous peoples. It is home to the spirits of ancestors, animals, and plants, all of which are respected and honored through ceremonies and rituals. This spiritual connection is a central aspect of Indigenous worldviews, where the land is seen as a living being that must be cared for and respected.

Ceremonies and rituals tied to the land are integral to the spiritual life of Indigenous communities. These practices reinforce the connection to the land and the responsibility to protect it for future generations. The spiritual connection to the land also provides a sense of continuity and resilience, helping Indigenous peoples maintain their identity and culture in the face of colonization and dispossession.

Social and Cultural Practices:

The land is the foundation of Indigenous social and cultural practices. It is where families gather, where knowledge is shared, and where traditions are passed down. The land provides the resources needed for these practices, whether it is the plants used in traditional medicine, the animals hunted for food, or the materials used in crafts and art.

The connection to the land is also reflected in the governance and social structures of Indigenous communities. Decisions about land use, resource management, and community development are often made collectively, with input from elders, knowledge keepers, and other community members. This ensures that the needs of the community are balanced with the health of the land and that traditional practices are maintained.

Resistance and Resilience:

The deep connection to the land has been a source of strength and resilience for Indigenous peoples in the face of colonization and dispossession. Despite the efforts of colonial governments to sever this connection, Indigenous peoples have maintained their ties to the land through resistance, cultural revival, and legal challenges.

Land-based movements, such as the reclamation of traditional territories and the protection of sacred sites, are expressions of this deep connection. These movements are not just about regaining control of land; they are about reasserting Indigenous identity, culture, and sovereignty. The resilience of Indigenous peoples in the face of ongoing threats to their land and culture is a testament to the enduring strength of this connection.

The Role of Land in Indigenous Cultures, Economies, and Governance Structures

Land is the foundation of Indigenous life, serving as the bedrock of culture, economy, and governance for the diverse nations that have inhabited what is now Canada for millennia. For Indigenous peoples, land is not just a physical space; it is a living entity with which they have a reciprocal relationship. It is the source of their spiritual beliefs, cultural practices, economic activities, and systems of governance. The intricate connection between land and these aspects of Indigenous life underscores the profound impact that land dispossession has had on Indigenous communities, as it strikes at the very core of their existence.

Land in Indigenous Cultures

For Indigenous peoples, land is central to cultural identity and expression. The land is not only where communities live and thrive but also where their stories, histories, and spiritual beliefs are rooted. The cultural significance of land is reflected in the oral traditions, ceremonies, and practices that have been passed down through generations, each one deeply connected to the landscapes and ecosystems that surround Indigenous communities.

Spiritual and Religious Significance:

In many Indigenous cultures, the land is considered sacred, imbued with the spirits of ancestors, animals, plants, and other beings. This spiritual connection to the land is a fundamental aspect of Indigenous worldviews, where the earth is seen as a living, breathing entity that must be respected and cared for. This respect is manifested in various ceremonies and rituals that honor the land and its resources, such as the potlatch of the Northwest Coast peoples, the Sun Dance of the Plains Nations, and the various seasonal ceremonies that mark the cycles of nature.

Sacred sites, such as mountains, rivers, and groves, hold special spiritual significance and are often the locations of important ceremonies and pilgrimages. These sites are not just places of worship; they are integral to the cultural and spiritual life of Indigenous communities. The desecration or loss of these sites through land dispossession and development has had a devastating impact on the cultural and spiritual continuity of Indigenous peoples.

Cultural Practices and Knowledge:

Indigenous cultural practices are deeply intertwined with the land and its resources. Traditional knowledge, which includes the skills and practices related to hunting, fishing, gathering, and agriculture, is rooted in a deep understanding of the environment. This knowledge is passed down through generations, often through oral traditions, stories, and hands-on learning. The land serves as both a classroom and a library, where knowledge is gained, preserved, and transmitted.

Cultural practices such as crafting, artwork, and the making of traditional clothing are also connected to the land. The materials used in
these practices—such as wood, bark, hides, and plants—are sourced
from the land, and the techniques used are often specific to the environment in which the community lives. These practices are not just about
survival; they are expressions of identity, creativity, and the relationship
between people and the land.

Language and Place Names:

Language is a critical component of culture, and for many Indigenous
peoples, their languages are deeply connected to the land. Place names,
in particular, reflect the significance of the land in Indigenous cultures.
These names often describe the landscape, its features, and its resources,
encoding valuable ecological knowledge and cultural stories. The loss of
land and the imposition of colonial place names have contributed to the
erosion of Indigenous languages and cultural connections to the land.
Revitalizing Indigenous languages is closely tied to land rights, as the
land provides the context and meaning for many of the words and concepts in these languages. Reclaiming land and restoring traditional place
names are acts of cultural renewal and resistance, reinforcing the connection between language, culture, and territory.

Land in Indigenous Economies

Land is not only central to Indigenous cultures but also to their
economies. Traditional economies were—and in many cases, continue
to be—based on the sustainable use of the land and its resources. These
economies were diverse, adaptive, and closely tied to the specific en-
vironments in which Indigenous communities lived. The loss of land
through colonization and the imposition of capitalist economic systems
have severely disrupted these traditional economies, leading to poverty
and economic marginalization in many Indigenous communities.

Subsistence and Sustainable Use:

Indigenous economies were traditionally based on a subsistence model,
where communities relied on hunting, fishing, gathering, and agriculture to meet their needs. These activities were governed by principles of

sustainability and respect for the natural world. For example, the Haida people of the Pacific Northwest managed their forests and fisheries with practices that ensured the long-term health of these resources, such as selective harvesting and the use of seasonal restrictions.

The sustainable use of resources was not only a practical necessity but also a cultural imperative. Indigenous peoples understood that the health of the land was directly tied to the health of their communities. Overharvesting or depleting resources was seen as a violation of the natural order and was actively discouraged through social norms and spiritual teachings.

Trade and Exchange:

Indigenous economies were not isolated; they were part of extensive trade networks that spanned vast distances across North America. These networks facilitated the exchange of goods such as furs, fish, agricultural products, and crafted items. The Wendat (Huron) Confederacy, for example, played a central role in the fur trade, acting as intermediaries between European traders and other Indigenous nations.

Trade was not solely an economic activity; it was also a means of establishing and maintaining social and political relationships between different nations. These relationships were often formalized through treaties, alliances, and marriage, creating a web of interconnected communities that were mutually supportive. The disruption of these trade networks through European colonization had profound economic and social consequences for Indigenous peoples.

Resource Management and Development:

Indigenous resource management practices were based on a deep understanding of local ecosystems and were designed to maintain the balance between human use and environmental health. This included the management of game populations, the cultivation of wild plants, and the maintenance of landscapes through practices such as controlled burning.

In recent years, there has been a resurgence of Indigenous-led resource management and economic development initiatives. These initiatives are often based on traditional knowledge and practices, combined with modern techniques and technologies. Indigenous communities are increasingly asserting their rights to manage and benefit from the resources on their lands, whether through forestry, mining, fishing, or tourism. These efforts represent a reclaiming of economic sovereignty and a return to the principles of sustainability that have always been central to Indigenous economies.

Land in Indigenous Governance Structures

Indigenous governance structures are deeply rooted in the land. The land provides the foundation for the laws, customs, and social organization of Indigenous nations. Governance was traditionally decentralized, with each community or nation managing its own territory according to its own laws and practices. The imposition of colonial governance systems disrupted these structures, but Indigenous peoples have continued to assert their inherent rights to self-governance, often centering their authority on their relationship with the land.

Territoriality and Jurisdiction:

Indigenous governance is inherently territorial, with each nation having jurisdiction over its own lands and resources. This territoriality is not just a matter of control over physical space but is tied to the responsibility to care for the land and its inhabitants. Indigenous laws and governance practices are designed to maintain the health and balance of the land, ensuring that it can continue to provide for future generations. The imposition of colonial borders and the reserve system fragmented Indigenous territories and undermined Indigenous governance. However, many Indigenous nations continue to assert their jurisdiction over their traditional territories, challenging the authority of colonial governments and seeking to restore their governance systems. This includes the establishment of Indigenous-led governance institutions, such as tribal councils and land management boards, which are based on traditional practices and principles.

Collective Decision-Making:

Indigenous governance structures are often based on principles of consensus and collective decision-making. Decisions about land use, resource management, and community development are made through consultation and dialogue, with input from elders, knowledge keepers, and other community members. This approach ensures that the needs of the community are balanced with the health of the land and that decisions are made in a way that reflects the values and priorities of the nation.

The role of elders and other knowledge keepers in governance is particularly important. These individuals are recognized for their wisdom, experience, and understanding of traditional laws and practices. Their guidance is essential in making decisions that are in harmony with the natural world and the long-term well-being of the community.

Sovereignty and Self-Determination:

The concept of sovereignty is central to Indigenous governance. For Indigenous peoples, sovereignty is not just a political concept but a recognition of their inherent rights to govern themselves and their lands. This sovereignty is rooted in their long-standing relationship with the land and their responsibilities to care for it.

The struggle for land rights is closely tied to the broader struggle for self-determination. Indigenous nations are increasingly asserting their sovereignty through legal challenges, political advocacy, and the establishment of self-governing agreements. These efforts are aimed at reclaiming control over their lands and resources and restoring their governance systems, which have been undermined by colonial policies.

Self-determination is also about the ability to make decisions that reflect the values, cultures, and priorities of Indigenous communities. This includes decisions about land use, economic development, and the preservation of cultural practices. By reclaiming their land and governance structures, Indigenous peoples are working towards a future where they can exercise their rights and responsibilities as sovereign nations.

First Contact and Early Relations with European Settlers

Initial Interactions Between Indigenous Peoples and European Settlers

The initial interactions between Indigenous peoples and European settlers marked the beginning of a profound and often tragic transformation of the land now known as Canada. These early encounters were characterized by a complex mix of curiosity, cooperation, and conflict, setting the stage for the long and fraught history that would follow. For Indigenous peoples, these encounters were not simply meetings between strangers; they were the beginning of a profound and often devastating disruption of their way of life, culture, and territorial sovereignty.

The Arrival of European Explorers

The first recorded contact between Indigenous peoples and Europeans in what is now Canada occurred with the arrival of Norse explorers in the late 10th century. However, these early visits, such as those led by Leif Erikson, were fleeting and did not lead to sustained interactions. It wasn't until the late 15th and early 16th centuries that European explorers began to arrive in greater numbers, driven by the quest for new trade routes and the search for valuable resources.

When John Cabot landed on the eastern shores of what is now Canada in 1497, he encountered the rich fishing grounds off Newfoundland, which soon attracted European fishing fleets. However, it was the arrival of Jacques Cartier in 1534 that marked the beginning of more sustained contact between Indigenous peoples and European settlers. Cartier's expeditions up the St. Lawrence River brought him into contact with the St. Lawrence Iroquoians, setting the stage for a new era of interaction.

For the Indigenous peoples of the region, these initial encounters with Europeans were marked by a mixture of curiosity and caution. The newcomers brought with them strange goods—metal tools, cloth, and beads—that were unlike anything the Indigenous peoples had seen before. These items were initially viewed with interest and were integrated into existing trade networks. However, the arrival of Europeans also brought new dangers, as the introduction of diseases like smallpox, for which Indigenous peoples had no immunity, led to devastating epidemics that would decimate entire communities.

The Fur Trade and Early Alliances

As European exploration expanded, the fur trade quickly became the dominant economic activity in the region. Indigenous peoples, particularly in the eastern woodlands and Great Lakes region, played a crucial role in this trade. They were expert trappers and traders, with extensive knowledge of the land and the animals that inhabited it. European demand for beaver pelts, which were used to make fashionable hats in Europe, led to the rapid expansion of the fur trade, drawing more European traders and settlers to the region.

The fur trade created new opportunities for Indigenous peoples, who initially viewed the Europeans as potential allies and trading partners. Early relations were often characterized by mutual benefit, as Indigenous peoples provided furs in exchange for European goods such as metal tools, firearms, and textiles. These goods were integrated into Indigenous economies and cultures, enhancing their ability to hunt, fish, and defend their territories.

However, the fur trade also brought new pressures and conflicts. As European demand for furs grew, competition between Indigenous groups increased, leading to shifts in traditional alliances and rivalries. The introduction of firearms further escalated conflicts, as groups vied for control of the fur trade and the territories rich in fur-bearing animals. The fur trade also began to alter traditional economies, as Indigenous peoples became more dependent on European goods and less focused on their traditional subsistence practices.

European powers quickly recognized the strategic importance of forming alliances with Indigenous nations. The French, in particular, established strong ties with the Huron-Wendat Confederacy, who controlled the fur trade routes between the Great Lakes and the St. Lawrence River. These alliances were often formalized through treaties, marriage, and the exchange of gifts, which were essential components of Indigenous diplomacy. The French also established trading posts and settlements, such as Quebec City in 1608, further cementing their presence in the region.

The English, who established their own colonies along the Atlantic coast, also sought alliances with Indigenous nations. The Iroquois Confederacy, who were rivals of the Huron-Wendat, became important allies of the English, particularly as tensions between the French and English in North America grew. These alliances were not simply opportunistic; they were deeply rooted in Indigenous political traditions, where alliances were based on reciprocity, mutual respect, and the exchange of gifts.

Cultural Exchange and Misunderstandings

The initial interactions between Indigenous peoples and European settlers were also marked by significant cultural exchange. Indigenous peoples shared their knowledge of the land, including hunting techniques, medicinal plants, and navigation, which were invaluable to the survival of European settlers in the harsh and unfamiliar environment. Indigenous guides and interpreters often played crucial roles in European exploration and trade, helping to bridge the cultural and linguistic divide.

However, these early interactions were also fraught with misunderstandings. The European concept of land ownership, which was based on individual property rights and the commodification of land, was fundamentally alien to Indigenous worldviews. For Indigenous peoples, land was not something to be owned or sold; it was a communal resource to be shared and respected. The failure of European settlers to understand this led to numerous conflicts and disputes over land, as settlers encroached on Indigenous territories and claimed land for themselves.

The arrival of Christian missionaries also introduced new cultural and religious dynamics. Missionaries, particularly the Jesuits, sought to convert Indigenous peoples to Christianity, often with little regard for existing spiritual beliefs and practices. While some Indigenous peoples adopted elements of Christianity, others resisted the efforts of the missionaries, leading to tensions and, in some cases, violent confrontations. The missionaries' efforts to undermine Indigenous spiritual practices were part of a broader pattern of cultural imperialism, where European settlers sought to impose their beliefs and values on the Indigenous peoples they encountered.

Conflict and Cooperation

Despite the opportunities for trade and alliance, the initial interactions between Indigenous peoples and European settlers were not without conflict. As more settlers arrived and began to establish permanent colonies, the demand for land increased, leading to encroachment on Indigenous territories. This encroachment often led to disputes and violence, as Indigenous peoples sought to defend their lands and way of life.

The French and English, who were the dominant European powers in the region, often found themselves drawn into these conflicts, either as participants or as mediators. The French, for example, supported their Huron-Wendat allies in their conflicts with the Iroquois, leading to a series of wars that would have devastating consequences for both Indigenous and European communities. The English, meanwhile, sought to expand their influence by supporting the Iroquois in their campaigns against French-allied nations.

These conflicts were not just about land and resources; they were also about power and control. Indigenous nations were not passive victims in these struggles; they were active participants who sought to protect their interests and assert their sovereignty. The alliances they formed with European powers were often strategic, designed to leverage European support in their own conflicts and to secure their positions in the rapidly changing landscape of North America.

Despite the conflicts, there were also moments of cooperation and mutual benefit. Indigenous peoples and European settlers often relied on each other for survival in the harsh conditions of the New World.

Indigenous knowledge of the land, plants, and animals was invaluable to the settlers, who were often unprepared for the realities of life in North America. In turn, European goods and technologies were integrated into Indigenous societies, enhancing their ability to adapt to the changing circumstances.

The Long-Term Impact of Early Interactions

The initial interactions between Indigenous peoples and European settlers set the stage for the complex and often contentious relationships that would develop over the following centuries. While these early encounters were marked by both cooperation and conflict, they ultimately led to the gradual dispossession of Indigenous lands and the erosion of Indigenous sovereignty.

The alliances that were formed during this period often proved to be double-edged swords for Indigenous peoples. While they provided short-term benefits, such as access to European goods and military support, they also tied Indigenous nations to the fortunes of their European allies. As European conflicts, such as the Seven Years' War, spilled over into North America, Indigenous nations found themselves drawn into a web of alliances and rivalries that often worked against their long-term interests.

The fur trade, which initially brought wealth and influence to Indigenous communities, also had long-term consequences. The depletion of fur-bearing animals, coupled with the growing dependence on European goods, weakened traditional economies and made Indigenous peoples increasingly vulnerable to the pressures of colonization. As European settlers expanded further into Indigenous territories, the demand for land grew, leading to the gradual encroachment on Indigenous lands and the displacement of Indigenous communities.

The cultural exchange that occurred during this period was also a double-edged sword. While it led to the enrichment of both Indigenous and European cultures, it also introduced new challenges, such as the spread of diseases, the imposition of European religious beliefs, and the erosion of Indigenous languages and traditions.

In conclusion, the initial interactions between Indigenous peoples and European settlers were complex and multifaceted, marked by both cooperation and conflict. These early encounters set the stage for the long and difficult history of colonization, dispossession, and resistance that would follow. Understanding these initial interactions is crucial for understanding the broader context of Indigenous-settler relations in Canada and the ongoing struggle for Indigenous rights and sovereignty.

Early Treaties and Agreements, and Their Significance in the Context of Land Rights

The history of early treaties and agreements between Indigenous peoples and European settlers is a crucial, though often misunderstood, aspect of Canada's colonial past. These treaties were not merely historical footnotes but foundational documents that have had lasting implications for land rights and Indigenous sovereignty. For Indigenous peoples, these treaties were sacred covenants meant to ensure mutual respect and coexistence. However, for the European settlers and later the Canadian government, these treaties often became tools for land acquisition and control, ultimately leading to the dispossession and marginalization of Indigenous communities.

The Nature of Early Treaties

The concept of treaties was not new to Indigenous peoples when Europeans arrived. Many Indigenous nations had long-standing traditions of negotiating agreements with neighboring tribes, often to establish peace, trade, and shared use of resources. These agreements were seen as binding, spiritual commitments, often marked by ceremonies and the exchange of gifts. The sanctity of these agreements was paramount, and breaking a treaty was considered not only a breach of trust but a violation of the natural and spiritual order.

When European settlers first began to establish a presence in what is now Canada, they quickly realized the importance of securing alliances with Indigenous nations. These alliances were often formalized through treaties, which were intended to ensure peaceful relations, facilitate trade, and, increasingly, secure land for European settlement. However, the understanding of these treaties differed significantly between the two parties. For Indigenous peoples, treaties were agreements to share the land and its resources, with each party maintaining its sovereignty and rights. For Europeans, treaties were often seen as legal instruments to assert control over land and resources, often at the expense of Indigenous sovereignty.

Key Early Treaties and Their Implications

The Peace and Friendship Treaties (1725-1779):

Among the earliest treaties in Canada were the Peace and Friendship Treaties, negotiated between the British Crown and the Mi'kmaq, Maliseet, and Passamaquoddy peoples of the Atlantic region. These treaties were not about land cession but about establishing peaceful relations and defining the terms of trade and alliance. The Indigenous signatories did not perceive these treaties as relinquishing their rights to land or sovereignty; rather, they were agreements to coexist and share resources.

The significance of these treaties lies in their recognition of Indigenous sovereignty and the absence of any clear land surrender. However, over time, the Crown began to reinterpret these agreements as having secured British control over the land, a perspective that would later fuel conflicts and contribute to the erosion of Indigenous land rights in the region.

The Royal Proclamation of 1763:

The Royal Proclamation of 1763, issued by King George III following the British victory in the Seven Years' War, is often considered a foundational document in the history of Indigenous land rights in Canada. The Proclamation recognized Indigenous land rights by prohibiting the sale of Indigenous lands to anyone other than the Crown. It also established a framework for the negotiation of future treaties, requiring that any land cessions be agreed upon through formal treaties with Indigenous nations.

While the Proclamation was intended to stabilize relations between settlers and Indigenous peoples and prevent further conflict, its implementation was far from consistent. In practice, the Crown often ignored its own regulations, allowing settlers to encroach on Indigenous lands without proper treaties. Nonetheless, the Proclamation is frequently cited in legal contexts as an acknowledgment of Indigenous land rights, even as the Crown systematically undermined these rights in the ensuing decades.

The Treaty of Niagara (1764):

The Treaty of Niagara, negotiated between the British Crown and over twenty Indigenous nations in 1764, was a significant extension of the principles outlined in the Royal Proclamation. The Treaty was meant to secure alliances with Indigenous nations in the aftermath of the Seven Years' War and the Pontiac's War, ensuring peace and mutual respect. The Treaty of Niagara included a symbolic exchange of wampum belts, which represented a binding, sacred commitment to the terms of the agreement.

The Indigenous nations understood the Treaty of Niagara as an affirmation of their sovereignty and a commitment to peaceful coexistence on their terms. However, as with other treaties, the British Crown later interpreted the agreement as granting them greater control over the land, leading to further conflicts and land encroachments.

The Numbered Treaties (1871-1921):

The Numbered Treaties, signed between the Canadian government and various Indigenous nations across the Prairies, the North, and parts of Ontario, represent a more systematic and large-scale effort to secure land for European settlement and resource extraction. These treaties were often negotiated under conditions of duress, with Indigenous leaders facing the harsh realities of declining bison populations, increasing settler encroachment, and the pressures of assimilation policies.

The Indigenous signatories of the Numbered Treaties believed they were entering into agreements that would protect their ways of life, ensure access to essential resources, and secure a future for their communities. In contrast, the Canadian government viewed these treaties as instruments for land acquisition, providing the legal framework for the expansion of the Canadian state.

The significance of the Numbered Treaties in the context of land rights is profound. These treaties are still in force today and are often at the center of legal battles over land claims and resource rights. Indigenous peoples continue to assert that these treaties were meant to establish a relationship of mutual respect and sharing, not to extinguish their rights to the land.

The Legacy of Early Treaties

The early treaties and agreements between Indigenous peoples and European settlers have had a lasting impact on the landscape of land rights in Canada. For Indigenous nations, these treaties were sacred commitments, meant to ensure peace, protect their lands, and secure their future. However, the colonial powers, driven by expansionist ambitions, frequently interpreted these treaties in ways that served their own interests, often at the expense of Indigenous peoples.

The legacy of these treaties is one of betrayal and broken promises. As European settlement expanded, the Crown and later the Canadian government systematically violated the terms of these treaties, encroaching on Indigenous lands, exploiting their resources, and undermining their sovereignty. The interpretation and implementation of these treaties were often skewed in favor of the settlers, leading to the gradual erosion of Indigenous land rights.

Despite these challenges, the treaties remain a crucial foundation for Indigenous land claims and legal struggles. Indigenous nations continue to assert that these agreements must be honored according to their original spirit and intent. In recent years, there has been a growing recognition of the importance of these treaties, not only as legal documents but as expressions of the ongoing relationship between Indigenous peoples and the Canadian state.

The early treaties and agreements between Indigenous peoples and European settlers are central to the history of land rights in Canada.

While these treaties were initially seen by Indigenous nations as guarantees of peace, coexistence, and mutual respect, they were often manipulated by colonial powers to justify land dispossession and the expansion of European settlement. The significance of these treaties lies not only in their historical context but in their enduring relevance to the struggles for Indigenous land rights and sovereignty today.

As Canada continues to grapple with the legacy of colonization, the need to revisit and reinterpret these treaties in a manner that respects Indigenous perspectives and sovereignty is more pressing than ever. The path to reconciliation must include a commitment to honoring these treaties as they were intended—a sacred agreement between nations to share the land and live in peace.

Chapter 2: The Colonial Land Grab

The French Regime and Seigneurial Land Grants

The Establishment of New France and the Distribution of Indigenous Lands to European Settlers

The establishment of New France and the subsequent distribution of Indigenous lands to European settlers is a pivotal chapter in the history of colonialism in North America. This period marked the beginning of a systematic process of land appropriation that would have profound and lasting impacts on Indigenous peoples. From the initial arrival of French explorers to the establishment of a colonial government, the distribution of land in New France was characterized by a deliberate and systematic approach to dispossessing Indigenous peoples and facilitating European settlement.

The Arrival of French Explorers

The arrival of French explorers in the early 17th century set the stage for a dramatic transformation of the North American landscape. Jacques Cartier's voyages in the 1530s and Samuel de Champlain's founding of Quebec in 1608 marked the beginning of French interest in the vast territories inhabited by Indigenous nations. The French were primarily motivated by the pursuit of fur trade, which required access to extensive tracts of land and waterways.

From the outset, the French approach to land acquisition differed somewhat from that of the British colonists. While the French were less aggressive in their initial land claims, they quickly engaged in negotiations with Indigenous peoples to secure trading rights and alliances. The French understood the necessity of maintaining good relations with Indigenous nations to facilitate their fur trading operations. However, these negotiations were often skewed in favor of the French, leading to an increasing encroachment on Indigenous lands.

The Seigneurial System

A key mechanism through which the French established control over land in New France was the seigneurial system. This system, introduced in 1627, was a form of land distribution that granted large tracts of land along rivers to seigneurs (landlords), who in turn could grant portions of their land to tenants. The seigneurial system was designed to encourage settlement and agricultural development, but it had significant implications for Indigenous land ownership and use.

The seigneurial grants were typically long, narrow strips of land extending from a riverbank, which allowed settlers to have access to water and fertile land. The distribution of these lands was carried out with little regard for existing Indigenous land use patterns or territorial claims. Indigenous peoples, who had traditionally used land in ways that were harmonious with their cultural and economic practices, were often displaced by the imposition of the seigneurial system.

The Scale of Land Distribution

The scale of land distribution in New France was substantial. Between 1627 and 1760, it is estimated that approximately 10,000 seigneuries were granted, covering an area ranging between 5 and 10 million acres (25,000 to 50,000 square kilometers). This massive land transfer was not only a land grab but also a means of establishing a colonial foothold in North America.

The French government's land distribution policies were aimed at solidifying control over the territory and encouraging settlement. The grants were typically made to French settlers, who were often given preferential access to the best and most economically viable land. Indigenous nations, who had long occupied and managed these lands, found themselves increasingly marginalized and pushed to less desirable areas.

The Impact on Indigenous Peoples

The impact of the French land distribution policies on Indigenous peoples was profound. Indigenous nations were systematically dispossessed of their ancestral lands, which were crucial to their traditional ways of life. The loss of land not only disrupted traditional hunting, fishing, and agricultural practices but also eroded the social and cultural fabric of Indigenous communities.

Indigenous peoples were often coerced into signing agreements that they did not fully understand or that were negotiated under duress. The treaties and agreements that accompanied land transfers were frequently ambiguous and did not adequately protect Indigenous interests. As a result, Indigenous nations were left with diminished territories and limited resources, exacerbating their vulnerability and dependence on European settlers.

The Transition to British Control

Following the British conquest of New France in 1763, the land distribution policies continued, albeit under British administration. The British government maintained and expanded upon the French practices, further entrenching colonial control over Indigenous lands. The shift in control from French to British rule did little to address the underlying issues of land dispossession and Indigenous marginalization.

The British government continued to grant land to settlers and facilitate the expansion of European settlement. The British approach, while somewhat different in administrative details, perpetuated the same patterns of land appropriation and disregard for Indigenous land rights. This continuity of land policies contributed to the ongoing struggle of Indigenous nations to reclaim and protect their traditional territories.

Conclusion

The establishment of New France and the distribution of Indigenous lands to European settlers marked the beginning of a systematic and expansive process of land appropriation that would have enduring consequences for Indigenous peoples. The seigneurial system, large-scale land grants, and subsequent British policies all contributed to the dispossession and marginalization of Indigenous communities. This period of history highlights the fundamental injustices that have shaped the relationship between Indigenous peoples and European settlers, setting the stage for the ongoing struggles for land rights and sovereignty in Canada.

As we reflect on this history, it is crucial to recognize the lasting impact of these early colonial policies on Indigenous communities. The land dispossession experienced by Indigenous peoples in New France was not an isolated incident but part of a broader pattern of colonial exploitation and control. Addressing the historical injustices and working towards meaningful reconciliation requires a deep understanding of this past and a commitment to correcting the ongoing inequities that continue to affect Indigenous nations today.

The Impact of Seigneurial Land Grants on Indigenous Communities in Quebec

The seigneurial land grants in Quebec, established during the French colonial period, represent a pivotal chapter in the history of land distribution and Indigenous dispossession in Canada. These grants, which spanned from the early 17th century until the British conquest in 1763, had profound and often devastating effects on the Indigenous communities of the region. The seigneurial system was not merely a method of land allocation; it was a tool of colonial dominance that reshaped the landscape and displaced Indigenous peoples.

The Seigneurial System: An Overview

Introduced in 1627 under the regime of Cardinal Richelieu, the seigneurial system was designed to promote agricultural settlement along the fertile river valleys of New France, particularly in what is now Quebec. Under this system, land was granted to seigneurs (landlords), who were responsible for developing the land and establishing a feudal-like system of tenure. These seigneurs, in turn, granted parcels of their land to habitants (settlers), who were expected to cultivate it and contribute to the colony's growth.

The seigneurial grants were typically long and narrow strips of land stretching from the riverbanks inland. This design was intended to ensure that each settler had access to river transportation and fertile land. While the system was effective in encouraging European settlement and agriculture, it was implemented with little regard for the existing Indigenous land use patterns and territorial claims.

Dispossession and Displacement

The impact of the seigneurial land grants on Indigenous communities in Quebec was profound and disruptive. Prior to European contact, Indigenous peoples in the region, including the Huron-Wendat, Algonquin, and Iroquois nations, had well-established systems of land use and management. Their territories were integral to their cultural practices, economic activities, and social structures.

The introduction of the seigneurial system resulted in the large-scale appropriation of these lands, often without the consent or consultation of Indigenous inhabitants. The French colonial government, focused on expanding its control and fostering agricultural development, largely ignored the rights and claims of Indigenous peoples. This resulted in the following significant impacts:

Loss of Ancestral Lands: The seigneurial grants covered vast tracts of land that had been traditionally used by Indigenous communities for hunting, fishing, and agriculture. As these lands were redistributed to European settlers, Indigenous peoples were systematically dispossessed of their ancestral territories. The loss of land disrupted their traditional ways of life and undermined their cultural and spiritual connections to the land.

Erosion of Traditional Practices: The seigneurial system imposed European concepts of land ownership and use, which were fundamentally at odds with Indigenous practices. Indigenous peoples, who had traditionally managed their lands through communal and sustainable practices, were forced to adapt to new systems that did not align with their cultural values. This erosion of traditional practices had long-term effects on their ability to maintain their cultural identity and economic stability.

Social and Economic Disruption: The displacement caused by the seigneurial grants led to social and economic disruptions within Indigenous communities. The loss of access to prime hunting and fishing grounds, combined with the forced relocation to less hospitable areas, severely impacted their ability to sustain their communities. This economic hardship contributed to social instability and increased dependence on European goods and trade.

Fragmentation of Territories: The seigneurial grants often resulted in the fragmentation of Indigenous territories. As European settlers established their holdings, Indigenous lands were increasingly fragmented and encircled by European settlements. This fragmentation undermined traditional land management practices and created barriers to the movement and cohesion of Indigenous communities.

Legal and Political Marginalization: The imposition of the seigneurial system also contributed to the legal and political marginalization of Indigenous peoples. The French colonial government did not recognize Indigenous land rights in any meaningful way, and the treaties or agreements made were often vague and biased. This marginalization set a precedent for future colonial policies that continued to undermine Indigenous sovereignty and self-determination.

Resistance and Adaptation

Despite the challenges posed by the seigneurial system, Indigenous communities in Quebec demonstrated remarkable resilience and adaptability. They engaged in various forms of resistance, including negotiating with French authorities and leveraging their strategic alliances to protect their interests. For example, some Indigenous nations entered into formal agreements or treaties with the French in an attempt to secure their rights and territories, although these agreements were frequently undermined by colonial policies.

Additionally, Indigenous communities adapted to the changing circumstances by developing new economic strategies and engaging in trade with European settlers. They capitalized on the fur trade and other economic opportunities created by European contact, using these interactions to assert their agency and influence in the colonial landscape.

Legacy and Ongoing Impact

The legacy of the seigneurial land grants continues to reverberate in contemporary Canada. The historical processes of land dispossession and displacement have had enduring effects on Indigenous communities in Quebec and beyond. The loss of ancestral lands and the disruption of traditional practices have contributed to ongoing challenges related to land rights, cultural preservation, and economic development.

Efforts to address these historical injustices and support Indigenous land rights are ongoing. The recognition of Indigenous land claims, the negotiation of land agreements, and the implementation of land restitution initiatives are important steps towards redressing the impacts of historical land dispossession. However, meaningful reconciliation requires a comprehensive understanding of the historical context and a commitment to addressing the legacy of colonialism in all its forms.

Conclusion

The establishment of New France and the seigneurial land grants had a profound and lasting impact on Indigenous communities in Quebec. The systematic appropriation of their lands, combined with the imposition of foreign land management systems, led to significant cultural, economic, and social disruptions. Understanding the historical context and the impact of these policies is crucial for addressing the ongoing challenges faced by Indigenous peoples and working towards a more equitable and just future. The legacy of the seigneurial system serves as a reminder of the need for continued efforts to recognize and respect Indigenous land rights and sovereignty in Canada.

The British Conquest and Land Distribution Policies

Shift in Land Ownership Following the British Conquest of Canada in 1763

The British conquest of Canada in 1763 marked a pivotal shift in land ownership and governance that had far-reaching consequences for Indigenous peoples and their territories. This transition from French to British control did not merely change the flags and rulers; it fundamentally altered the land management practices, legal frameworks, and territorial boundaries that had long governed the region. The effects of this shift on Indigenous communities were profound and often detrimental, setting the stage for further dispossession and marginalization.

The Treaty of Paris 1763: A New Order

The Treaty of Paris, signed in 1763, formally ended the Seven Years' War and ceded French territories in North America to British control. This treaty was a turning point, as it reshaped the geopolitical landscape of the continent. While the British Crown gained control over vast expanses of territory, the implications for Indigenous peoples were largely ignored or inadequately addressed.

Redefinition of Boundaries: The Treaty of Paris redefined territorial boundaries, transferring control of New France to Britain. This new political reality meant that Indigenous territories, previously governed under French rule, were now subject to British laws and policies. The British Crown inherited the complex network of Indigenous relationships and land claims that had existed under French rule but chose to prioritize colonial expansion and settlement over Indigenous rights and sovereignty.

British Land Policies: The British government sought to consolidate its control over the newly acquired territories by implementing policies that would facilitate colonial expansion and settlement. This included the issuance of land grants and the establishment of new land management systems that were heavily biased against Indigenous interests.

British land policies often disregarded the existing Indigenous land use practices and traditional territories, leading to increased dispossession.

Land Grants and Settlement Policies

Following the conquest, the British Crown implemented a series of land grants and settlement policies designed to encourage European settlement and secure British control over the territories. These policies had significant consequences for Indigenous communities:

Land Grants to Loyalists: In the wake of the American Revolutionary War, the British government granted land to Loyalists who had fled the newly independent United States. These grants were often substantial and were distributed in areas that were traditionally occupied or used by Indigenous peoples. The influx of Loyalist settlers further encroached upon Indigenous lands and exacerbated the displacement of Indigenous communities.

The Proclamation of 1763: The Royal Proclamation of 1763 was issued to establish a framework for the administration of British North America and to address some of the concerns related to Indigenous land rights. The Proclamation recognized Indigenous land rights and attempted to establish boundaries between colonial and Indigenous lands. However, its implementation was inconsistent, and the Crown's commitment to upholding Indigenous land rights was often undermined by colonial and settler interests. The Proclamation established the principle that only the Crown could purchase Indigenous lands, but this principle was frequently ignored in practice.

Expansion and Settlement: The British government encouraged the expansion of settlements westward into Indigenous territories. This expansion was driven by economic interests and the desire to secure strategic and resource-rich lands. The influx of settlers and the establishment of new communities disrupted Indigenous land use patterns, further eroding their traditional territories.

Impact on Indigenous Communities

The shift in land ownership and governance following the British conquest had profound and often devastating effects on Indigenous communities:

Increased Dispossession: The British land policies and settlement practices led to a significant increase in land dispossession for Indigenous peoples. Traditional territories were increasingly encroached upon, and Indigenous communities were forced to cede their lands through treaties or agreements that were often made under duress or through coercion.

Legal and Political Marginalization: The British legal and political systems marginalized Indigenous peoples, disregarding their traditional governance structures and land management practices. The imposition of British laws and policies further eroded Indigenous autonomy and self-determination.

Economic Disruption: The loss of land had severe economic consequences for Indigenous communities. The displacement from traditional hunting, fishing, and agricultural lands disrupted their economic systems and led to increased dependence on European goods and trade. The economic instability contributed to social and cultural disruptions within Indigenous communities.

Cultural and Social Impact: The erosion of traditional territories and the imposition of foreign land management systems had a profound impact on Indigenous cultures and social structures. The loss of land disrupted traditional practices and governance, leading to long-term cultural and social consequences.

Resistance and Adaptation

Despite the challenges posed by British land policies and settlement practices, Indigenous communities continued to resist and adapt to the changing circumstances. They engaged in various forms of resistance, including negotiating with British authorities, forming alliances with other Indigenous nations, and advocating for their rights through legal and political channels.

Negotiations and Treaties: Indigenous communities negotiated treaties with the British Crown in an attempt to secure their land rights and establish agreements for land use and governance. While some treaties recognized Indigenous land rights, many were ambiguous or poorly implemented, leading to continued disputes and conflicts.

Strategic Alliances: Indigenous nations formed strategic alliances with other Indigenous groups and with European powers to protect their interests and resist encroachment. These alliances played a crucial role in maintaining their sovereignty and advocating for their rights.

Legal and Political Advocacy: In the face of ongoing dispossession and marginalization, Indigenous communities pursued legal and political avenues to assert their rights and challenge unjust land policies. This advocacy has continued into the present day, with ongoing efforts to secure land restitution, recognize Indigenous sovereignty, and address the legacy of colonialism.

Legacy and Ongoing Issues

The shift in land ownership following the British conquest of Canada in 1763 had a lasting impact on Indigenous communities and their relationship with the land. The dispossession, marginalization, and disruption caused by British policies set a precedent for future land management practices and colonial policies. Understanding this historical context is crucial for addressing the ongoing challenges faced by Indigenous peoples and working towards meaningful reconciliation and justice.

The legacy of British land policies and the impact of colonialism continue to shape the landscape of Indigenous land rights and sovereignty in Canada. Efforts to address these historical injustices and support Indigenous land claims are ongoing, with a focus on recognizing and respecting Indigenous rights, restoring traditional territories, and promoting self-determination.

Conclusion

The shift in land ownership following the British conquest of Canada in 1763 marked a significant turning point in the history of

Indigenous dispossession and colonial expansion. The imposition of British land policies and settlement practices had profound and often devastating effects on Indigenous communities. Understanding this historical context is essential for addressing the legacy of colonialism and working towards a more equitable and just future for Indigenous peoples in Canada. The ongoing efforts to recognize Indigenous land rights and support land restitution are crucial steps in the process of reconciliation and justice.

The British System of Land Grants and Sales, and Its Effects on Indigenous Land Holdings

The British system of land grants and sales, implemented after their conquest of Canada in 1763, profoundly affected Indigenous land holdings and governance. This system was designed to encourage European settlement, bolster the British colonial economy, and secure territorial control. Unfortunately, it systematically undermined Indigenous land rights, leading to significant loss of territory and disruption of traditional ways of life.

British Land Grant Policies

Land Grants to Loyalists and Settlers: Following the American Revolutionary War, the British government sought to reward Loyalists who had supported the Crown by providing them with land in the newly acquired territories of Canada. These land grants were extensive and often located in regions traditionally occupied by Indigenous peoples. Loyalists were given substantial tracts of land, often ranging from 100 to several thousand acres. This distribution significantly encroached upon Indigenous territories, displacing many communities from their ancestral lands.

Systematic Land Sales: In addition to land grants, the British government implemented a system of land sales to encourage further settlement. Land was sold at low prices to settlers and speculators, who were often given large parcels of land. The sale of land was driven by the British government's desire to promote economic development and consolidate control over the territory. This system of land sales facilitated the rapid expansion of European settlements, further diminishing Indigenous land holdings.

Royal Proclamation of 1763: The Royal Proclamation of 1763 was issued to establish administrative guidelines for British North America and address some of the issues related to Indigenous land rights. The Proclamation attempted to create a boundary between colonial and Indigenous lands and recognized Indigenous land rights, stating that only the Crown could purchase Indigenous lands. However, the implementation of this proclamation was inconsistent, and the Crown frequently ignored or undermined its principles in favor of colonial and settler interests.

Impact on Indigenous Land Holdings

Encroachment and Dispossession: The British land grant and sales policies led to significant encroachment on Indigenous lands. As settlers moved into these newly granted and purchased lands, Indigenous communities were often forcibly removed or pushed into smaller, less productive areas. The expansion of European settlements disrupted traditional land use practices and led to widespread dispossession of Indigenous territories.

Disruption of Traditional Systems: Indigenous communities had well-established systems of land management and use that were deeply intertwined with their cultural and social practices. The British land policies disrupted these systems, as traditional territories were divided and allocated without regard for Indigenous ways of life. This disruption had severe consequences for Indigenous economies and social structures, leading to increased dependency on European goods and services.

Economic and Social Impacts: The loss of land had profound economic and social impacts on Indigenous communities. Traditional economic activities such as hunting, fishing, and agriculture were severely affected by the loss of land. The encroachment on Indigenous territories also led to increased competition for resources and exacerbated social tensions. Indigenous communities were often forced into reliance on government aid or European trade, further undermining their traditional ways of life.

Legal and Political Marginalization: The British system of land grants and sales marginalized Indigenous peoples legally and politically. The imposition of British land management systems and laws disregarded Indigenous governance structures and land rights. Indigenous communities were often excluded from legal negotiations and decisions regarding their lands, further entrenching their marginalization.

Resistance and Adaptation

Negotiation and Legal Action: In response to the encroachment and dispossession, Indigenous communities engaged in negotiations with the British Crown to protect their land rights. Some communities sought to establish treaties or agreements to secure their territories and rights. However, many of these agreements were inadequately implemented or ignored by the Crown, leading to ongoing disputes and conflicts.

Cultural and Social Adaptation: Despite the challenges posed by British land policies, Indigenous communities adapted to the changing circumstances in various ways. They sought to preserve their cultural practices and social structures while navigating the new realities imposed by colonialism. This included forming alliances with other Indigenous nations and pursuing strategies to assert their rights and protect their lands.

Continued Advocacy: The legacy of British land policies continues to impact Indigenous communities today. Ongoing advocacy and legal action aim to address historical injustices and secure land restitution. Indigenous communities are actively engaged in efforts to reclaim their lands, assert their rights, and promote reconciliation.

Subscribed

The Role of the Royal Proclamation of 1763

The Royal Proclamation of 1763 as a Legal Framework for Land Transactions

The Royal Proclamation of 1763 stands as a foundational document in the history of land management in Canada. Issued by King George III, it was intended to regulate land transactions and address the complex issues arising from British colonial expansion. Despite its noble intentions, the Proclamation has had a mixed legacy, particularly concerning its impact on Indigenous land rights and relations.

Background and Intent

Context of the Proclamation: The Royal Proclamation was issued in the wake of the British victory in the Seven Years' War and the subsequent acquisition of French territories in North America. The British government faced the challenge of integrating these new territories while managing relations with Indigenous peoples who had long occupied these lands. The Proclamation aimed to establish a framework for governance, land management, and diplomatic relations with Indigenous nations.

Purpose of the Proclamation: The Proclamation's primary objectives were to:

Create a clear boundary between British colonial settlements and Indigenous territories to reduce conflicts.

Recognize and formalize Indigenous land rights by requiring that any land transfers be conducted through the Crown.

Prevent colonial encroachment on Indigenous lands by restricting settlement west of the Appalachian Mountains.

Key Provisions of the Proclamation

Land Cession and the Crown's Role: One of the Proclamation's most significant provisions was the assertion that only the Crown had the authority to purchase or acquire land from Indigenous peoples. This was intended to prevent settlers from negotiating land deals directly with Indigenous nations, thereby ensuring that all land transactions were formalized and regulated by the British government.

Boundary Line: The Proclamation established a boundary line, known as the "Proclamation Line," which was intended to separate colonial settlements from Indigenous territories. This boundary stretched from the Gulf of St. Lawrence down to the Mississippi River, aiming to limit colonial expansion into the western territories. The intention was to protect Indigenous lands from encroachment and reduce the potential for conflict.

Governance and Settlement: The Proclamation established new colonial governance structures in the newly acquired territories. It created a framework for administering justice, managing land, and establishing new colonies. Settlers were encouraged to move into these territories, but only within the boundaries defined by the Proclamation.

Implementation and Impact

Inconsistent Application: Despite its intent, the implementation of the Proclamation was inconsistent and often ignored. Colonial governments and settlers frequently violated the Proclamation's boundaries and negotiated land deals without the Crown's consent. This led to widespread encroachment on Indigenous lands and undermined the Proclamation's protective measures.

Disregard for Indigenous Sovereignty: The Proclamation recognized Indigenous land rights in principle, but in practice, it often disregarded Indigenous sovereignty and governance structures. Many Indigenous communities were not adequately consulted about the boundaries or the terms of land transactions. The Proclamation's promise to protect Indigenous lands was frequently undermined by colonial interests and policies that prioritized settlement and economic development over Indigenous rights.

Long-Term Consequences: The Proclamation's legacy is mixed. While it set a precedent for recognizing Indigenous land rights, its implementation fell short of its goals. The ongoing violation of the Proclamation's provisions contributed to the continued dispossession of Indigenous lands and strained relations between Indigenous communities and the Crown. The Proclamation's failure to prevent encroachment and its inconsistent enforcement laid the groundwork for many of the disputes and conflicts that continue to this day.

Legal and Historical Significance

Precedent for Treaty Negotiations: The Royal Proclamation established a legal precedent for treaty negotiations between the Crown and Indigenous nations. It recognized that Indigenous peoples had rights to their lands and that these rights could only be transferred through formal agreements with the Crown. This framework influenced subsequent treaty-making processes and negotiations.

Modern Relevance: The principles of the Royal Proclamation continue to be relevant in modern discussions about Indigenous land rights and sovereignty. Legal interpretations of the Proclamation have played a role in shaping Canadian law and policies related to Indigenous land claims and rights. Court cases and legal challenges have often referenced the Proclamation as a historical foundation for asserting Indigenous rights. Ongoing Reconciliation Efforts: In contemporary Canada, the Royal Proclamation is often cited in discussions about reconciliation and land restitution. Efforts to address historical injustices and affirm Indigenous rights frequently reference the Proclamation as a starting point for understanding the legal and historical context of land claims.

Implications for Indigenous Land Rights and Subsequent Violations by Settlers and Colonial Governments

The Royal Proclamation of 1763 was a groundbreaking document in the realm of colonial governance and Indigenous rights. On paper, it set out a framework that recognized Indigenous land rights and established a legal mechanism for land transactions. However, its practical implications were fraught with challenges and were marred by significant violations by settlers and colonial governments. This section delves into the Proclamation's intended protections for Indigenous land rights, the subsequent violations, and the enduring consequences for Indigenous communities.

Intended Protections and Recognition of Land Rights

Recognition of Indigenous Land Rights: The Proclamation aimed to affirm the recognition of Indigenous peoples' rights to their ancestral lands. By declaring that only the Crown had the authority to negotiate land purchases, it was supposed to safeguard Indigenous territories from unilateral land grabs by settlers. This provision was meant to prevent the erosion of Indigenous land holdings and ensure that any land transactions were conducted in a formal, regulated manner.

Establishment of the Proclamation Line: The Proclamation Line was intended to create a clear boundary between Indigenous territories and colonial settlements. This boundary was designed to prevent settlers from encroaching upon Indigenous lands and to respect Indigenous sovereignty over their traditional territories. The Proclamation sought to reduce conflict between settlers and Indigenous communities by establishing a demarcated area for each group.

Regulation of Land Transactions: By requiring that all land transactions be conducted through the Crown, the Proclamation aimed to prevent settlers from making unauthorized land deals with Indigenous peoples. This regulation was meant to ensure that land transfers were handled transparently and fairly, with the Crown acting as an intermediary to protect Indigenous interests.

Violations by Settlers and Colonial Governments

Settler Encroachment: Despite the Proclamation's clear intentions, settlers frequently ignored its boundaries and encroached upon Indigenous lands. The promise of land and opportunity drove many settlers to move westward, disregarding the Proclamation Line. This led to widespread violations of the Proclamation and encroachment on Indigenous territories, often resulting in conflict and displacement for Indigenous communities.

Illegal Land Deals: Colonial governments and settlers engaged in numerous illegal land deals that bypassed the Crown's authority. Settlers negotiated land purchases directly with Indigenous peoples without official sanction, undermining the Proclamation's intent to centralize and regulate land transactions. These unauthorized deals often resulted in unfair terms for Indigenous communities and contributed to the erosion of their land holdings.

Government Inaction and Inconsistency: The British colonial administration's enforcement of the Proclamation was inconsistent and often lax. Colonial authorities frequently failed to uphold the Proclamation Line or address violations by settlers. This lack of enforcement allowed settlers to expand into Indigenous territories with relative impunity, further undermining the Proclamation's protective measures.

Expansion of Colonial Territories: As colonial ambitions expanded, the boundaries set by the Proclamation were frequently disregarded or modified. The British government's desire to encourage settlement and economic development often took precedence over the Proclamation's protections for Indigenous lands. This led to the expansion of colonial territories into areas that were supposed to be reserved for Indigenous peoples.

Displacement and Dispossession: The combined effects of settler encroachment, illegal land deals, and government inaction led to the displacement and dispossession of Indigenous communities. Many Indigenous peoples were forced off their traditional lands, resulting in the loss of their homes, resources, and cultural practices tied to their territories. This dispossession had profound social, economic, and cultural impacts on Indigenous communities.

Enduring Consequences for Indigenous Communities

Cultural and Social Disruption: The loss of ancestral lands and the disruption of traditional land use practices had severe cultural and social consequences for Indigenous communities. The displacement from their territories undermined their traditional ways of life, leading to the erosion of cultural practices, social structures, and community cohesion.

Economic Marginalization: The dispossession of land contributed to the economic marginalization of Indigenous communities. Without access to their traditional lands and resources, many Indigenous peoples faced economic hardships and were dependent on government assistance. The loss of land also diminished opportunities for economic development and self-sufficiency.

Legal and Political Struggles: The violations of the Royal Proclamation set the stage for ongoing legal and political struggles over Indigenous land rights. Indigenous communities have been involved in numerous legal battles to assert their land claims and seek redress for historical injustices. The Proclamation's failure to protect Indigenous lands has led to a legacy of unresolved land disputes and ongoing negotiations with the Canadian government.

Reconciliation and Land Restitution Efforts: In recent years, the Royal Proclamation has become a symbol in discussions about reconciliation and land restitution. Efforts to address historical injustices and recognize Indigenous land rights often reference the Proclamation as a starting point. The Proclamation's mixed legacy underscores the need for meaningful reconciliation and the restoration of Indigenous land rights.

Chapter 3: The Expansion of the Canadian State The

The Expansion of the Canadian State
The Railway Boom and the Dominion Lands Act

The Role of Railway Expansion in the Further Dispossession of Indigenous Lands

The expansion of railways across Canada was one of the most transformative developments in the country's history, reshaping its economic and geographical landscape. However, this expansion also played a critical role in the dispossession of Indigenous lands, contributing to the erosion of traditional territories and exacerbating the marginalization of Indigenous communities. This section explores how railway expansion facilitated land dispossession, its impact on Indigenous peoples, and the broader implications for Canada's land policies.

Railway Expansion and Land Grants

Government Incentives for Railway Construction: In the late 19th and early 20th centuries, the Canadian government actively promoted railway expansion as a means of connecting the vast and diverse regions of the country. Recognizing the strategic and economic importance of railways, the government offered substantial land grants to railway companies as incentives to build rail lines. These grants were often in the form of large tracts of land adjacent to the railway routes.

Size and Scope of Land Grants: The scale of land grants was significant. Railway companies were granted extensive areas of land, often ranging from 20 to 40 sections (12,800 to 25,600 acres) per mile of track laid. In Western Canada alone, it is estimated that approximately 25 million acres (100,000 square kilometers) were allocated to railway companies between 1880 and 1920. This land, much of which was part of Indigenous territories, was transferred from public ownership to private control, drastically altering land distribution.

Impact on Indigenous Lands: The allocation of land to railway companies had a direct impact on Indigenous territories. Much of the land granted for railway construction was previously occupied or used by Indigenous communities. The establishment of railway lines often encroached upon traditional hunting grounds, fishing areas, and agricultural lands. This not only displaced Indigenous peoples but also disrupted their traditional ways of life and resource management practices.

The Dispossession Process

Encroachment and Displacement: As railways expanded, they brought an influx of settlers and economic activities to previously remote areas. The presence of railways facilitated easier access to Indigenous lands, leading to increased encroachment by settlers. Indigenous communities were often forced off their lands to make way for railway construction and the subsequent influx of settlers, leading to widespread displacement and loss of traditional territories.

Land Redistribution and Homesteading: The completion of railway lines opened up previously inaccessible lands for homesteading and settlement. The Canadian government encouraged settlement in these areas through policies like the Dominion Lands Act, which offered land to settlers at minimal costs. This land redistribution process largely excluded Indigenous peoples, who were systematically denied the opportunity to claim or benefit from the lands being made available to new settlers.

Government and Railway Company Interests: The interests of the government and railway companies often took precedence over the rights of Indigenous peoples. The drive for economic development and expansion led to the prioritization of railway construction and settlement over Indigenous land rights. The government's focus on facilitating economic growth and integrating the western territories into the national economy resulted in the marginalization of Indigenous concerns and the further dispossession of their lands.

Consequences for Indigenous Communities

Cultural Disruption: The encroachment and displacement resulting from railway expansion had profound cultural impacts on Indigenous communities. The loss of traditional lands disrupted Indigenous cultural practices, including hunting, fishing, and ceremonies tied to specific landscapes. The severing of these cultural ties contributed to a loss of identity and heritage for many Indigenous peoples.

Economic Marginalization: The displacement of Indigenous communities and the loss of traditional lands had severe economic consequences. Indigenous peoples were often forced into dependency on government assistance and were excluded from the economic opportunities that the railway expansion brought to settler communities. The economic marginalization of Indigenous communities persisted long after the completion of the railways.

Environmental Impact: The construction and operation of railways had significant environmental impacts on Indigenous lands. The disruption of ecosystems, deforestation, and the alteration of waterways affected the natural resources that Indigenous communities relied upon. The environmental degradation resulting from railway expansion further compounded the challenges faced by Indigenous peoples.

Legal and Political Struggles: The legacy of land dispossession due to railway expansion has led to ongoing legal and political struggles for Indigenous communities. Many Indigenous groups have sought redress for the injustices they suffered, including legal battles to reclaim land or secure compensation for losses incurred due to railway construction. These struggles highlight the long-lasting effects of historical policies and practices on Indigenous land rights.

Legacy and Reconciliation Efforts

Acknowledgment of Historical Injustices: The historical injustices associated with railway expansion have been increasingly acknowledged in recent years. Efforts to recognize and address these injustices are part of broader reconciliation initiatives aimed at addressing the wrongs committed against Indigenous communities and working towards repairing relationships.

Land Claims and Settlements: In response to historical land dispossession, there have been efforts to negotiate land claims and settlements with Indigenous communities. These negotiations often involve addressing grievances related to railway expansion and seeking compensation or land restitution as part of reconciliation efforts.

Ongoing Advocacy: Indigenous advocacy groups continue to push for recognition of the impacts of railway expansion and other forms of dispossession. Their efforts aim to ensure that historical injustices are addressed and that Indigenous land rights are respected in future development projects.

Land Grants to Railway Companies and Settlers Under the Dominion Lands Act

The Dominion Lands Act, enacted in 1872, was a cornerstone of Canada's land policy during the late 19th and early 20th centuries. It was designed to promote settlement and development of Western Canada by providing land to settlers. This policy, however, had far-reaching implications for Indigenous lands and communities, contributing significantly to their dispossession and marginalization. This section explores how the Dominion Lands Act facilitated land grants to railway companies and settlers, and the broader consequences for Indigenous peoples.

The Dominion Lands Act: An Overview

Purpose and Objectives: The Dominion Lands Act aimed to encourage settlement and agricultural development in the Western provinces of Canada, particularly in areas that were previously part of Indigenous territories. The Act provided a legal framework for distributing land to individuals willing to farm and improve it, with the goal of populating and developing the vast expanses of the Prairies and beyond.

Key Provisions: Under the Dominion Lands Act, individuals could apply for a quarter-section of land, equivalent to 160 acres, provided they met certain requirements. These included living on the land for a minimum of three years and making improvements such as building a dwelling and cultivating crops. The Act offered land at nominal costs or even for free, making it an attractive opportunity for settlers from various backgrounds.

Land Grants to Settlers Under the Dominion Lands Act

Encouraging Settlement and Agricultural Development: The Dominion Lands Act was instrumental in encouraging settlement in Western Canada. By offering land to settlers at minimal costs, the Act aimed to populate the region with agricultural communities. Settlers from various backgrounds, including European immigrants, took advantage of this opportunity to establish farms and communities on land that was often part of Indigenous territories.

Homesteading Requirements: To obtain land under the Dominion Lands Act, settlers were required to fulfill specific homesteading obligations. This included residing on the land for at least three years, building a dwelling, and cultivating a portion of the land. While these requirements were intended to ensure that the land was used productively, they also served to solidify settler claims to the land and marginalize Indigenous land use practices.

Consequences for Indigenous Communities: The distribution of land to settlers under the Dominion Lands Act had severe consequences for Indigenous communities. As settlers established farms and communities, Indigenous peoples were increasingly displaced from their traditional lands. The influx of settlers, facilitated by the land grants, led to the fragmentation of Indigenous territories and the disruption of traditional ways of life. Indigenous communities were often excluded from the land distribution process and were left to contend with the consequences of settler expansion.

Legal and Policy Framework

Legal Justifications and Dispossession: The legal framework established by the Dominion Lands Act and associated policies was used to justify the dispossession of Indigenous lands. The government's focus on settlement and agricultural development often took precedence over the rights and interests of Indigenous peoples. The legal justification for land transfers to settlers and railway companies was rooted in a policy of assimilation and integration, which disregarded Indigenous land rights and governance systems.

Impact on Treaty Rights and Agreements: The land grants made under the Dominion Lands Act and the associated policies had implications for existing treaties and agreements with Indigenous communities. Many of these treaties were signed under duress or with limited understanding of their long-term impacts. The widespread land grants to settlers and railway companies often violated the spirit of these treaties and undermined the agreements made with Indigenous peoples.

Historical and Ongoing Grievances: The legacy of land dispossession resulting from the Dominion Lands Act and related policies continues to be a source of grievance for Indigenous communities. Legal battles and negotiations have sought to address these historical wrongs, with varying degrees of success. The ongoing struggle for land rights and recognition reflects the enduring impact of the policies implemented during this period.

Consequences and Legacy

Cultural and Economic Impact: The dispossession of Indigenous lands due to land grants to settlers and railway companies had profound cultural and economic impacts. The loss of traditional lands disrupted Indigenous cultural practices and economic activities. Indigenous communities faced challenges in maintaining their cultural heritage and traditional knowledge in the face of increasing encroachment and settlement.

Environmental Degradation: The expansion of agriculture and settlement under the Dominion Lands Act also led to environmental degradation in many areas. The alteration of landscapes, deforestation, and changes in land use affected ecosystems and natural resources that Indigenous communities relied upon. The environmental impact of settler expansion contributed to the broader consequences of land dispossession.

Ongoing Struggles for Land Rights: The legacy of land dispossession has led to ongoing struggles for land rights and recognition. Indigenous communities continue to advocate for the return of lands, compensation, and the restoration of their rights. The historical injustices associated with land grants and settlement policies are central to contemporary discussions about reconciliation and justice.

The Establishment of Reserves and the Exclusion of Indigenous Peoples from the Homesteading Process

The establishment of reserves and the exclusion of Indigenous peoples from the homesteading process are pivotal chapters in the history of land dispossession in Canada. These policies not only marginalized Indigenous communities but also institutionalized their displacement from their traditional territories. This section delves into how reserves were established, the systemic exclusion of Indigenous peoples from land opportunities, and the broader implications of these practices.

The Establishment of Reserves

Origins and Rationale: The reserve system was established in the late 19th century as part of a broader strategy to control and manage Indigenous lands and peoples. The government's rationale for creating reserves was to consolidate Indigenous populations into designated areas, ostensibly to protect their traditional ways of life while simultaneously facilitating European settlement and economic development in other parts of the country.

Implementation and Legislation: The Indian Act of 1876 was instrumental in formalizing the reserve system. Under this legislation, Indigenous peoples were confined to small parcels of land known as reserves. These lands were often selected based on their limited agricultural potential or economic value, ensuring that the best lands were available for European settlers. The reserve system was designed to undermine Indigenous sovereignty and restrict their traditional land use practices.

Land Allocation and Size: The size and quality of reserve lands varied significantly, with many reserves being established on lands that were unsuitable for agriculture or other economic activities. The allocation of reserve lands was often done without meaningful consultation with Indigenous communities, and the lands were frequently chosen based on their marginal value compared to the lands offered to settlers.

Impact on Indigenous Communities: The establishment of reserves disrupted Indigenous communities by forcing them onto smaller, less productive lands. This disruption had severe consequences for traditional land use practices, such as hunting, fishing, and gathering, which were integral to the cultural and economic life of many Indigenous groups. The reserve system also led to a loss of autonomy and control over traditional territories.

Exclusion from the Homesteading Process

Homesteading Opportunities for Settlers: The Dominion Lands Act provided settlers with the opportunity to claim and develop land in Western Canada. Homesteading was a key policy for promoting agricultural settlement and economic development in the region. Settlers were granted land under relatively easy terms, provided they fulfilled certain requirements, such as living on the land and improving it.

Systematic Exclusion of Indigenous Peoples: Indigenous peoples were systematically excluded from the homesteading process. The legal and policy framework of the time did not recognize Indigenous land rights in the same way it recognized settler claims. Indigenous peoples were not allowed to participate in the homesteading process, and their traditional lands were often appropriated without consent or compensation. Barriers to Participation: Several factors contributed to the exclusion of Indigenous peoples from the homesteading process. The Indian Act and other legislation explicitly restricted Indigenous peoples from claiming land under homesteading policies. Additionally, many Indigenous communities were confined to reserves, which were not eligible for homesteading. The bureaucratic and legal obstacles faced by Indigenous peoples prevented them from accessing land opportunities that were readily available to settlers.

Legal and Policy Justifications: The legal and policy justifications for excluding Indigenous peoples from homesteading were rooted in a broader agenda of assimilation and control. The government's policies were designed to assimilate Indigenous peoples into European ways of life while simultaneously exploiting their traditional lands for settler use. These policies assumed that Indigenous peoples were incapable of effectively managing or benefiting from the lands in the same way as settlers.

Broader Implications and Consequences

Cultural and Economic Disruption: The exclusion of Indigenous peoples from the homesteading process had significant cultural and economic repercussions. The loss of traditional lands and the imposition of reserve systems disrupted Indigenous ways of life, including cultural practices, economic activities, and social structures. The confinement to reserves limited economic opportunities and hindered the development of Indigenous communities.

Long-Term Impact on Indigenous Rights: The legacy of exclusion and dispossession has had long-term effects on Indigenous rights and sovereignty. The reserve system and the denial of land opportunities have contributed to ongoing struggles for land rights and recognition. The historical injustices experienced by Indigenous communities continue to influence contemporary efforts to address grievances and achieve justice.

Contemporary Reconciliation Efforts: In recent years, there has been increasing recognition of the need to address historical wrongs and work towards reconciliation with Indigenous communities. Efforts to rectify past injustices include land claims settlements, legal battles for land rights, and policy reforms aimed at improving the socio-economic conditions of Indigenous peoples. However, meaningful reconciliation remains a complex and ongoing process.

The Indian Act and Its Impact on Land Ownership

The Creation and Implementation of the Indian Act

The Indian Act of 1876 stands as one of the most controversial and consequential pieces of legislation in Canadian history, fundamentally shaping the relationship between the Canadian government and Indigenous peoples. Its creation and implementation mark a pivotal moment in the systematic control and regulation of Indigenous communities, reflecting a broader agenda of assimilation and domination. This section explores the origins, provisions, and impacts of the Indian Act, illustrating how it was instrumental in consolidating colonial control over Indigenous lands and cultures.

Origins of the Indian Act

Historical Context: The Indian Act was introduced during a period of intense colonial expansion and consolidation in Canada. By the late 19th century, the Canadian government sought to assert control over Indigenous lands and populations as part of a broader strategy to facilitate European settlement and economic development. The Indian Act was conceived as a tool to manage and control Indigenous affairs, formalize land policies, and impose a framework of governance that aligned with colonial interests.

Legislative Background: The Indian Act was drafted by the federal government under the guidance of Indian Affairs officials, who sought to create a legal framework for managing Indigenous communities. The legislation was influenced by existing colonial policies and practices that aimed to assimilate Indigenous peoples into European ways of life. The Act consolidated and codified previous laws and regulations related to Indigenous peoples, centralizing authority and control in the federal government.

Purpose and Objectives: The primary objectives of the Indian Act were to control and regulate various aspects of Indigenous life, including land management, governance, and cultural practices. The Act was designed to enforce a European-style system of governance and legal norms upon Indigenous communities, undermining traditional systems of governance and cultural practices. The overarching aim was to assimilate Indigenous peoples into the dominant settler society and reduce their cultural and political autonomy.

Provisions of the Indian Act

Reserve System: The Indian Act formalized and expanded the reserve system, which had been established through previous policies. Reserves were designated lands where Indigenous peoples were to be relocated, often on lands that were less desirable for agricultural or economic activities. The Act stipulated that reserves were to be managed by Indian Affairs officials, further centralizing control over Indigenous lands.

Governance and Leadership: The Indian Act introduced a system of governance for Indigenous communities that imposed a chief and council structure, replacing traditional governance systems. The Act outlined the powers and responsibilities of these elected leaders, but also restricted their authority and autonomy. The system was designed to align with colonial administrative practices and diminish the influence of traditional Indigenous leaders.

Cultural and Social Controls: The Act included provisions that sought to control and suppress Indigenous cultural practices and social structures. This included regulations on ceremonies, traditional practices, and the use of Indigenous languages. The Indian Act aimed to replace

THE
Indigenous cultural practices with European norms, reinforcing the agenda of assimilation.

Land and Resource Management: The Indian Act centralized control over Indigenous lands and resources in the federal government. It imposed restrictions on land use and transfer, and established a system of land management that often ignored Indigenous needs and rights. The Act also facilitated the exploitation of resources on reserve lands by granting the government authority to lease or sell these resources.

Legal and Administrative Authority: The Indian Act granted the federal government broad legal and administrative powers over Indigenous communities. This included the authority to regulate various aspects of Indigenous life, such as education, health care, and welfare. The Act created a bureaucratic system for managing Indigenous affairs, further entrenching colonial control.

Implementation and Impact

Enforcement and Administration: The Indian Act was enforced through the Department of Indian Affairs, which administered and managed Indigenous affairs on behalf of the federal government. Indian Affairs officials were responsible for implementing the provisions of the Act, including the administration of reserves, governance structures, and cultural regulations. The enforcement of the Act was often carried out with little regard for the needs or perspectives of Indigenous communities.

Cultural Suppression: The Indian Act's provisions aimed at suppressing Indigenous cultures and traditions had profound and damaging effects on Indigenous communities. Traditional practices, languages, and social structures were undermined by the Act's regulations, leading to significant cultural loss and disruption. The imposition of European norms and values contributed to the erosion of Indigenous cultural identities.

Resistance and Adaptation: Despite the oppressive nature of the Indian Act, Indigenous communities have demonstrated remarkable resilience and adaptability. Many communities resisted the Act's provisions and sought to maintain their cultural practices and governance systems. Over time, Indigenous peoples have also worked to challenge and reform aspects of the Indian Act, advocating for greater autonomy and recognition of their rights.

Legal and Political Challenges: The Indian Act has faced ongoing criticism and legal challenges from Indigenous communities and advocates. Various legal battles have sought to address the injustices and limitations imposed by the Act, including efforts to assert land rights, challenge discriminatory provisions, and promote self-governance. The Act remains a focal point in discussions about Indigenous rights and reconciliation.

Contemporary Reforms and Discussions: In recent years, there have been efforts to reform or replace the Indian Act in response to calls for greater self-determination and respect for Indigenous rights. These discussions involve exploring alternatives to the Act that better reflect the needs and aspirations of Indigenous communities. The process of reform is complex and ongoing, requiring meaningful consultation and collaboration with Indigenous leaders and communities.

How the Act Reinforced the Reserve System and Restricted Indigenous Land Ownership

The Indian Act of 1876 was a cornerstone of colonial policy aimed at controlling and managing Indigenous peoples in Canada. One of its most significant impacts was the reinforcement of the reserve system and the imposition of restrictive measures on Indigenous land ownership. This section delves into how the Indian Act entrenched the reserve system, limited Indigenous land ownership, and facilitated ongoing colonial control over Indigenous lands.

Reinforcement of the Reserve System

Codification of Reserve Lands: The Indian Act formalized and codified the reserve system that had been established through earlier policies and treaties. Under the Act, reserves were designated lands where Indigenous peoples were to be relocated and concentrated. This codification provided a legal framework for managing these lands and ensured that reserve lands were controlled by federal authorities, rather than being subject to local or traditional Indigenous governance.

Centralized Control: The Act centralized control over reserve lands in the federal government, specifically the Department of Indian Affairs. This centralization allowed the government to dictate the administration and management of reserves, including decisions about land use, allocation, and governance. Indigenous communities had limited authority over their own lands, as decisions were made by federal officials rather than by the communities themselves.

Size and Location of Reserves: The Indian Act established criteria for the size and location of reserves, which often resulted in lands that were inadequate for sustaining traditional ways of life. Reserves were frequently located on less desirable lands, such as marginal agricultural areas or regions with limited resources. This strategic placement ensured that the most valuable lands and resources were reserved for European settlers and economic development, while Indigenous communities were left with minimal and often suboptimal lands.

Regulation of Reserve Boundaries: The Act also gave the federal government the authority to alter reserve boundaries and relocate reserves if deemed necessary. This flexibility allowed the government to adjust reserve lands according to its own interests, often at the expense of Indigenous communities. Such changes disrupted traditional land use and further undermined Indigenous control over their territories.

Restrictions on Indigenous Land Ownership

Impediments to Private Land Ownership: The Indian Act prohibited Indigenous peoples from owning land privately. All reserve lands were considered "Crown land," meaning they were owned by the federal government and controlled by Indian Affairs. Indigenous communities could not sell, lease, or transfer reserve lands without government approval. This restriction prevented Indigenous peoples from engaging in land transactions and acquiring private property, significantly limiting their economic opportunities.

Lease and Sale of Lands: The Act allowed the federal government to lease or sell reserve lands to third parties, often without the full consent of the affected Indigenous communities. Leases and sales of reserve lands were typically conducted for the benefit of non-Indigenous entities, such as railway companies, mining interests, or agricultural enterprises. Indigenous communities had little say in these transactions, which frequently led to the exploitation and depletion of their resources.

Management of Land Resources: The Indian Act gave the federal government control over the management of land resources on reserves. This included oversight of natural resources, such as timber, minerals, and water. The government often prioritized economic development and resource extraction over the interests and needs of Indigenous communities. This control restricted Indigenous peoples' ability to manage and benefit from their own resources.

Restrictions on Indigenous Economic Development: The Act's restrictions on land ownership and resource management also hindered Indigenous economic development. By limiting access to land and resources, the Act created significant barriers to economic growth and self-sufficiency for Indigenous communities. This impediment to economic development was a deliberate aspect of the broader colonial strategy to maintain control over Indigenous populations.

Enfranchisement and Land Grants: The Act included provisions for enfranchisement, which allowed Indigenous peoples to become "full citizens" of Canada by renouncing their status as Indians. Enfranchised individuals could apply for land grants, but these were often inadequate and failed to compensate for the loss of their traditional lands. The enfranchisement process was used as a means to further undermine Indigenous land rights and assimilate Indigenous peoples into Euro-Canadian society.

Impact and Legacy

Cultural Disruption: The reinforcement of the reserve system and restrictions on land ownership had profound cultural impacts on Indigenous communities. Traditional land use practices, cultural ceremonies, and social structures were disrupted by the imposition of reserve boundaries and European-style governance. The reserve system contributed to the erosion of Indigenous cultures and the loss of traditional knowledge and practices.

Economic Disadvantage: The restrictions imposed by the Indian Act created significant economic disadvantages for Indigenous communities. Limited access to land and resources hindered economic development and perpetuated cycles of poverty and dependence on government assistance. The inability to engage in land transactions or resource management further marginalized Indigenous communities from the broader economic system.

Resistance and Advocacy: Despite the restrictive nature of the Indian Act, Indigenous communities have demonstrated resilience and resistance. Many communities have sought to assert their land rights, challenge discriminatory provisions, and advocate for greater autonomy. Legal battles, advocacy efforts, and political activism have been central to efforts to reform or replace the Indian Act and achieve justice for Indigenous peoples.

Ongoing Challenges: The legacy of the Indian Act continues to shape the experiences of Indigenous communities in Canada. The reserve system and restrictions on land ownership remain significant issues in discussions about Indigenous rights and reconciliation. Addressing these challenges requires a comprehensive understanding of the historical context and a commitment to meaningful reform.

The Legacy of the Indian Act in Contemporary Land Rights Issues

The Indian Act of 1876 remains one of the most enduring symbols of colonial control and discrimination against Indigenous peoples in Canada. Although it has been amended over the years, its foundational principles and impacts continue to shape contemporary land rights issues. This section explores the legacy of the Indian Act in relation to current land rights struggles, highlighting how historical injustices continue to affect Indigenous communities today.

Continued Centralization and Control

Federal Authority Over Lands: The Indian Act centralized control over reserve lands within the federal government, specifically the Department of Indian Affairs, now known as Indigenous Services Canada. This centralization persists, as the federal government maintains authority over the administration and management of reserve lands. Indigenous communities often face bureaucratic hurdles and delays when attempting to manage or develop their own lands, illustrating the continued influence of colonial control.

Restrictive Land Management: Under the Indian Act, all reserve lands are classified as "Crown land," which means they are owned by the federal government. Indigenous communities must navigate complex regulations and obtain government approval to undertake land transactions, development projects, or resource extraction. This regulatory burden hinders the ability of communities to effectively manage and utilize their lands, perpetuating economic disadvantages and limiting opportunities for self-determination.

Limited Autonomy: The Indian Act's restrictions on private land ownership and control over resources significantly limit the autonomy of Indigenous communities. While some communities have negotiated agreements or self-government arrangements to gain more control, the overall structure established by the Act still exerts significant influence. The lack of full land ownership and the ongoing need for federal approval for many land-related activities reflect a persistent erosion of Indigenous self-governance and decision-making power.

Impact on Economic Development

Economic Marginalization: The restrictions imposed by the Indian Act have contributed to the economic marginalization of Indigenous communities. Limited access to land and resources, coupled with bureaucratic obstacles, has hindered economic development and perpetuated cycles of poverty. Many communities continue to struggle with inadequate infrastructure, limited economic opportunities, and dependence on government assistance, all of which stem from historical policies entrenched by the Indian Act.

Barriers to Resource Development: Indigenous communities seeking to develop natural resources on their lands face significant challenges due to the Indian Act's restrictions. The need for federal approval and the requirement to lease lands rather than own them outright create barriers to capital investment and resource extraction. This has resulted in missed economic opportunities and diminished benefits from resource development projects, which are often pursued by external companies with limited benefits returning to the communities.

Unequal Access to Compensation: Enfranchisement provisions and compensation schemes established under the Indian Act have often been inadequate or unfair. Indigenous individuals who were enfranchised faced significant losses, including the loss of traditional land rights and inadequate compensation. The legacy of these inequitable arrangements continues to impact communities seeking redress and fair compensation for historical injustices.

Ongoing Legal and Political Struggles

Legal Challenges and Reforms: Indigenous communities have pursued legal challenges to address the limitations imposed by the Indian Act. Landmark cases, such as those involving land claims and resource rights, have sought to assert Indigenous rights and challenge discriminatory practices. While some legal victories have been achieved, the process of securing justice and achieving meaningful reform remains complex and arduous.

Calls for Reform or Abolition: There is widespread recognition among Indigenous leaders and advocates that the Indian Act is fundamentally flawed and requires significant reform or outright abolition. Efforts to replace or amend the Act have been met with varying degrees of success, but the overarching goal remains to dismantle the colonial structures imposed by the Act and establish more equitable and self-determined systems of governance for Indigenous communities.

Political Advocacy: Political advocacy for land rights and self-determination continues to be a central focus for Indigenous organizations and leaders. Advocacy efforts aim to challenge the enduring impacts of the

Indian Act, promote legislative changes, and support initiatives that enhance Indigenous autonomy and land management. These efforts are crucial in addressing contemporary land rights issues and advancing reconciliation.

Cultural and Social Impacts

Disruption of Traditional Practices: The Indian Act's imposition of reserve boundaries and restrictions on land use have disrupted traditional Indigenous practices and ways of life. The loss of access to traditional lands, hunting grounds, and sacred sites has had profound cultural and social impacts, affecting the ability of Indigenous communities to maintain their cultural heritage and practices.

Cultural Resilience and Revival: Despite the challenges posed by the Indian Act, Indigenous communities have demonstrated remarkable resilience and determination in preserving and revitalizing their cultures. Efforts to reclaim traditional practices, languages, and governance structures reflect a strong commitment to cultural continuity and self-determination, even in the face of historical and ongoing obstacles.

Intergenerational Trauma: The legacy of the Indian Act is intertwined with the broader context of intergenerational trauma experienced by Indigenous communities. Historical injustices, including forced relocation, cultural suppression, and systemic discrimination, have had lasting effects on Indigenous individuals and communities. Addressing these impacts requires a comprehensive approach that acknowledges and addresses the historical and ongoing trauma resulting from colonial policies

Chapter 4: The Modern Era of Dispossession

Post-Confederation Land Policies

Continued Land Transfers and the Marginalization of Indigenous Communities

The history of land transfers in Canada is marked by a relentless pattern of dispossession and marginalization of Indigenous communities. Despite numerous treaties and agreements, the continued transfer of land to non-Indigenous interests and the ongoing marginalization of Indigenous peoples reveal a systemic disregard for Indigenous land rights and sovereignty. This section examines how these continued land transfers perpetuate historical injustices and further entrench the marginalization of Indigenous communities.

Ongoing Land Transfers

Historical Context of Land Transfers: Land transfers have been a cornerstone of colonial policies in Canada, systematically stripping Indigenous communities of their ancestral lands. From early European settlement through the establishment of reserves, to modern land deals and resource development, the pattern of transferring land to non-Indigenous entities has persisted. These transfers have often occurred without proper consent or fair compensation for the displaced communities, reflecting a disregard for Indigenous rights and sovereignty.

Modern Land Deals and Resource Development: In contemporary

times, the transfer of land for resource development projects remains a significant issue. Large-scale mining, forestry, and oil and gas projects often proceed on lands claimed by Indigenous communities, frequently without adequate consultation or consent. The federal and provincial governments, along with private corporations, continue to prioritize economic gains over Indigenous rights, leading to conflicts and disputes over land use and ownership.

Legal and Administrative Challenges: The legal framework governing land transfers often fails to protect Indigenous interests adequately. Despite legal obligations for consultation and accommodation, these processes are frequently superficial, with governments and corporations proceeding with projects regardless of Indigenous opposition. The administrative challenges faced by Indigenous communities, including bureaucratic hurdles and limited resources, further exacerbate their marginalization in land transfer negotiations.

Impact on Indigenous Communities

Economic Marginalization: The continued transfer of land away from Indigenous control has significant economic implications for affected communities. The loss of land restricts access to traditional economic activities such as hunting, fishing, and gathering, which are integral to Indigenous economies and cultural practices. Moreover, the exclusion from resource development projects means that Indigenous communities miss out on potential economic benefits, perpetuating cycles of poverty and dependency.

Cultural Displacement: Land is not merely a physical asset for Indigenous peoples; it is deeply intertwined with their cultural, spiritual, and social practices. Continued land transfers disrupt traditional practices, displace communities from their ancestral territories, and erode cultural connections to the land. This displacement impacts the ability of Indigenous peoples to maintain their cultural heritage and practices, leading to a loss of identity and cultural continuity.

Environmental Consequences: The environmental degradation resulting from land transfers and resource extraction projects has severe consequences for Indigenous communities. The destruction of landscapes, pollution of waterways, and depletion of natural resources undermine the health and well-being of communities who rely on these ecosystems for sustenance and cultural practices. The lack of meaningful environmental protections and oversight in land transfer agreements exacerbates these impacts, further marginalizing Indigenous communities.

Systemic Inequities

Disproportionate Impact: Indigenous communities are disproportionately affected by land transfers and resource development projects compared to non-Indigenous communities. The systemic inequities inherent in land transfer processes reflect broader patterns of marginalization and discrimination. Indigenous communities often lack the political power and resources to effectively advocate for their interests, resulting in unequal treatment and ongoing injustices.

Inadequate Compensation: When land is transferred for development or other purposes, the compensation offered to Indigenous communities is frequently inadequate. Monetary compensation or token benefits do not account for the full value of the land, the loss of cultural connections, or the long-term environmental impacts. This inadequate compensation further entrenches economic disparities and perpetuates the marginalization of Indigenous peoples.

Lack of Real Consultation: Consultation processes related to land transfers are often criticized for being perfunctory and insincere. Indigenous communities are frequently presented with projects as faits accomplis, with limited opportunities to influence outcomes or negotiate meaningful benefits. The lack of genuine consultation undermines Indigenous self-determination and reinforces the power imbalance between Indigenous communities and government or corporate entities.

Resistance and Advocacy

Legal Challenges and Court Cases: Indigenous communities have pursued legal challenges to contest land transfers and assert their rights. Landmark court cases, such as those involving land claims, treaty rights, and environmental protections, have sought to address injustices and secure recognition of Indigenous sovereignty. These legal battles highlight the ongoing struggle for justice and the need for systemic change.

Advocacy and Activism: Indigenous leaders and activists continue to advocate for greater control over land and resources, pushing for reforms and policy changes that address historical and ongoing injustices. Advocacy efforts focus on demanding meaningful consultation, fair compensation, and respect for Indigenous land rights. These efforts play a crucial role in raising awareness and driving change in land transfer policies and practices.

Community-Led Initiatives: In addition to external advocacy, many Indigenous communities are taking proactive steps to reclaim and manage their lands. Community-led initiatives, such as land reclamation projects, cultural revitalization programs, and economic development ventures, reflect a commitment to self-determination and resilience. These initiatives demonstrate the capacity of Indigenous communities to overcome historical marginalization and forge a path toward a more equitable future.

The Role of Federal and Provincial Governments in Controlling Land and Resources

The control of land and resources in Canada has long been a domain predominantly managed by federal and provincial governments, often to the detriment of Indigenous communities. This centralized control reflects a historical and ongoing power dynamic where government authorities exert significant influence over land use and resource allocation, frequently sidelining Indigenous rights and interests. This section explores how federal and provincial governments maintain control over land and resources, and the impacts this control has on Indigenous communities.

Historical Foundations of Government Control

Colonial Origins: The control of land and resources by colonial authorities laid the groundwork for modern governance in Canada. European settlers and colonial governments established systems to regulate land ownership, use, and resource extraction, often without regard for

Indigenous land rights. The imposition of these systems effectively marginalized Indigenous governance structures and laid the foundation for ongoing disputes over land and resource management.

Confederation and Expansion: Following Confederation in 1867, the federal government assumed control over vast tracts of land and resources across Canada. The expansion westward was facilitated by policies that prioritized settlement and resource development, often at the expense of Indigenous land rights. The establishment of reserves, the imposition of the Indian Act, and the granting of land to railway companies and settlers exemplify how federal control was exerted over Indigenous territories.

Federal Government's Role

Legislative Authority: The federal government wields significant legislative authority over land and resource management through various acts and policies. The Indian Act, the Canadian Environmental Assessment Act, and other federal regulations establish the framework for land use and resource extraction, often prioritizing economic development over Indigenous rights. These legislative tools grant the federal government the power to control and regulate lands that are crucial to Indigenous communities.

Resource Management and Development: Federal policies regarding resource management and development frequently favor industry interests, resulting in significant environmental and social impacts. The federal government has historically granted licenses and permits for mining, oil and gas extraction, and other resource activities on lands that Indigenous communities claim. These decisions are often made without adequate consultation or accommodation of Indigenous interests, leading to conflicts and disputes.

Land Transfers and Settlements: The federal government plays a central role in land transfers and settlement agreements with Indigenous communities. Although there have been efforts to address historical injustices through land claims and treaty negotiations, the process is often slow, bureaucratic, and marked by unequal power dynamics. Federal control over land transfers and settlement outcomes can limit the effectiveness of these agreements and perpetuate ongoing grievances.

Provincial Government's Role

Land Use Planning and Zoning: Provincial governments have significant authority over land use planning and zoning within their jurisdictions. This includes the ability to allocate land for various purposes such as agriculture, industry, and residential development. Provincial policies and decisions on land use can directly impact Indigenous communities, particularly when it comes to resource extraction and development projects that affect their traditional territories.

Resource Development and Revenue: Provincial governments often oversee the development and management of natural resources, including forestry, mining, and energy resources. They grant permits and licenses for resource extraction and collect revenue from these activities. The focus on maximizing economic benefits from resource development can overshadow the rights and interests of Indigenous communities, who are frequently excluded from the decision-making process.

Environmental Regulations: Provinces are responsible for enforcing environmental regulations related to land and resource use. While these regulations are intended to protect the environment, they can sometimes be insufficient or inadequately enforced, leading to environmental degradation that disproportionately affects Indigenous communities. The provincial approach to environmental protection often lacks meaningful engagement with Indigenous perspectives and traditional ecological knowledge.

Impacts on Indigenous Communities

Disenfranchisement and Marginalization: The centralized control of land and resources by federal and provincial governments contributes to the disenfranchisement and marginalization of Indigenous communities. Indigenous peoples are often excluded from decision-making processes that affect their traditional lands and resources, resulting in limited opportunities for participation and influence. This exclusion reinforces power imbalances and perpetuates historical injustices.

Environmental and Cultural Consequences: The impacts of government-controlled resource development and land use on Indigenous communities are profound. Environmental degradation resulting from mining, logging, and other industrial activities disrupts traditional ways of life and threatens cultural practices. The destruction of ecosystems and contamination of waterways undermine the health and well-being of Indigenous communities, further marginalizing their voices and rights.

Economic Disparities: Indigenous communities frequently face economic disparities as a result of government control over land and resources. The exclusion from resource development projects and the limited benefits derived from land use result in economic disadvantages. The concentration of economic gains from resource extraction in non-Indigenous hands exacerbates poverty and inequality within Indigenous communities.

Legal and Political Challenges

Challenges to Sovereignty: The control exercised by federal and provincial governments often conflicts with Indigenous claims to sovereignty and self-determination. Legal battles and political struggles over land rights highlight the ongoing tension between government authority and Indigenous self-governance. These challenges underscore the need for reforms that respect Indigenous sovereignty and address systemic inequalities.

Ineffective Consultation Processes: Consultation processes regarding land and resource management are frequently criticized for being superficial and inadequate. The lack of meaningful engagement with Indigenous communities and the failure to address their concerns contribute to ongoing conflicts and disputes. Effective consultation requires a genuine partnership approach that respects Indigenous rights and incorporates their perspectives into decision-making.

Calls for Reform: Indigenous leaders and advocates continue to call for reforms to address the inequities in land and resource control. Efforts include demands for greater self-determination, equitable resource sharing, and meaningful consultation processes. These calls for reform reflect the need for systemic change to rectify historical injustices and ensure that Indigenous communities have a fair role in managing their lands and resources.

Contemporary Land Disputes and Legal Challenges

Key Legal Battles Over Land and Resource Rights

Indigenous land and resource rights in Canada have been the subject of numerous legal battles, as Indigenous nations seek to assert their rights and challenge historical injustices. These key legal cases highlight the struggle for recognition and respect of Indigenous land rights and the ongoing conflict between Indigenous claims and government policies. This section examines three significant legal battles: the Tsilhqot'in Nation, Innu Nation, and Ktunaxa Nation cases.

Tsilhqot'in Nation v. British Columbia (2014)

Background: The Tsilhqot'in Nation, a group of six First Nations in British Columbia, embarked on a legal battle to assert their rights to a vast area of traditional territory. The case, known as Tsilhqot'in Nation v. British Columbia, was initiated in response to the British Columbia government's granting of logging licenses and resource extraction permits within Tsilhqot'in territory without the Nation's consent.

Supreme Court Ruling: In 2014, the Supreme Court of Canada delivered a landmark decision in favor of the Tsilhqot'in Nation. The Court recognized the Tsilhqot'in's claim to Aboriginal title over a significant portion of their traditional territory, making it the first time the Supreme Court granted Indigenous title to a specific area of land. This ruling confirmed that the Tsilhqot'in had never ceded their rights to the land and were entitled to control over its use.

Implications: The Tsilhqot'in decision set a precedent for the recognition of Aboriginal title and significantly impacted land and resource management in Canada. The ruling affirmed that Indigenous nations have the right to control their lands, make decisions about resource development, and benefit from the resources within their territories. It also highlighted the need for meaningful consultation and consent before any development occurs on Indigenous lands.

Challenges: Despite the victory, the Tsilhqot'in Nation continues to face challenges in fully realizing their land rights. Ongoing disputes with the provincial government and industry over resource development and land use highlight the difficulties in implementing the Supreme Court's decision and addressing historical grievances.

Innu Nation v. Canada (2019)

Background: The Innu Nation, located in Labrador and Quebec, has long been engaged in a legal struggle to assert their rights over traditional lands affected by resource development. The case, Innu Nation v. Canada, centered around the impact of the Upper Churchill hydroelectric project on Innu lands and the failure of the federal government to adequately consult and accommodate the Innu Nation's interests.

Supreme Court Ruling: In 2019, the Supreme Court of Newfoundland and Labrador ruled in favor of the Innu Nation. The Court found that the federal government had failed to fulfill its duty to consult and accommodate the Innu Nation regarding the development of the Upper Churchill project. The ruling emphasized that the government must engage in meaningful consultation and take into account the potential impacts on Indigenous rights and interests.

Implications: The Innu Nation decision underscored the importance of consultation and accommodation in the context of resource development. The ruling reinforced the duty of the federal government to engage with Indigenous communities and address their concerns before proceeding with projects that affect their traditional territories. It also highlighted the need for fair compensation and consideration of Indigenous rights in development decisions.

Challenges: While the ruling was a significant victory for the Innu Nation, the challenges of implementing the decision and addressing the impacts of past resource development remain. The Innu Nation continues to advocate for greater recognition of their rights and more equitable benefits from resource development projects on their lands.

Ktunaxa Nation v. British Columbia (2017)

Background: The Ktunaxa Nation, an Indigenous group in British Columbia, challenged the development of a proposed ski resort on their traditional territory, which they consider a sacred site. The legal battle, Ktunaxa Nation v. British Columbia, focused on the duty to consult and accommodate the Ktunaxa's religious and cultural rights in relation to the project.

Supreme Court Ruling: In 2017, the Supreme Court of Canada ruled against the Ktunaxa Nation, finding that the British Columbia government had met its duty to consult and accommodate the Ktunaxa's concerns about the development. The Court concluded that while the government had a duty to consider the Ktunaxa's spiritual beliefs, it was not obligated to fully align its decisions with those beliefs.

Implications: The Ktunaxa decision highlighted the limits of the duty to consult and accommodate in protecting Indigenous cultural and spiritual rights. The ruling raised questions about the extent to which government consultation processes must respect Indigenous values and beliefs. It also emphasized the challenges of balancing economic development with the protection of sacred and culturally significant sites.

Challenges: The Ktunaxa Nation's struggle to protect their sacred site from development underscores the ongoing tension between economic interests and Indigenous rights. Despite the legal setback, the Ktunaxa Nation continues to advocate for the protection of their cultural heritage and the recognition of their rights in land and resource decisions.

The Role of the Courts in Shaping Indigenous Land Rights in Canada

The Canadian judiciary has played a pivotal role in shaping the landscape of Indigenous land rights. Through landmark rulings and evolving legal principles, Canadian courts have both challenged and upheld various aspects of Indigenous land claims and rights. This section explores the influence of the courts on Indigenous land rights, examining key legal doctrines, significant rulings, and the broader implications of judicial decisions.

Historical Context and Legal Doctrines

Doctrine of Discovery: The Doctrine of Discovery, introduced by European colonial powers, posited that lands "discovered" by European explorers were claimed by the Crown. This doctrine laid the groundwork for the dispossession of Indigenous lands. While not a legal doctrine in the modern sense, its legacy has influenced Canadian land rights issues, shaping early legal frameworks and policies.

Royal Proclamation of 1763: The Royal Proclamation established a framework for land transactions between the Crown and Indigenous peoples, recognizing Indigenous land rights and requiring treaties for land cessions. Though often violated, the Proclamation remains a foundational document in understanding Indigenous land rights within Canadian law.

The Sparrow Test (1986): The Supreme Court's decision in R v. Sparrow established the legal framework for determining whether government actions infringe upon Indigenous rights. The Sparrow Test requires that any infringement on Indigenous rights must be justified by a compelling and substantial objective and must be implemented in a manner consistent with the honor of the Crown.

Key Court Cases and Their Implications

Calder v. British Columbia (1973): The Calder case was groundbreaking in recognizing that Indigenous land rights existed prior to European contact. The Supreme Court acknowledged the Nisga'a Nation's claim to their traditional lands and established that Aboriginal title had legal standing, setting a precedent for future land claims.

Implications: Calder marked the beginning of a new era in Canadian jurisprudence, affirming the existence of Aboriginal title and prompting the government to negotiate land claims and treaties with Indigenous nations. It was a significant step toward recognizing and validating Indigenous land rights within the Canadian legal system.

R v. Van der Peet (1996): This case clarified the legal test for determining the existence of Aboriginal rights under section 35 of the Constitution Act, 1982. The Supreme Court established that Indigenous practices must be integral to the distinctive culture of the community to be protected under section 35.

Implications: The Van der Peet decision refined the criteria for recognizing Aboriginal rights and emphasized the importance of cultural continuity and significance in land claims. It provided a framework for assessing and validating Indigenous practices and rights in the context of contemporary legal standards.

Delgamuukw v. British Columbia (1997): The Delgamuukw case reaffirmed the existence of Aboriginal title and clarified the legal requirements for proving such title. The Supreme Court emphasized that oral histories and traditional knowledge are valid sources of evidence in land claims.

Implications: Delgamuukw enhanced the recognition of oral histories and Indigenous knowledge in legal proceedings. It reinforced the need for governments to respect Indigenous land rights and provided a clearer understanding of the nature and scope of Aboriginal title.

Mikisew Cree First Nation v. Canada (2005): The Mikisew Cree case addressed the duty to consult and accommodate Indigenous communities when making decisions that affect their rights. The Supreme Court ruled that the Crown has a constitutional duty to consult Indigenous peoples regarding decisions that impact their rights and interests.

Implications: The ruling established the duty to consult as a legal obligation, requiring the Crown to engage with Indigenous communities and consider their concerns in decision-making processes. This decision has had a profound impact on resource development and land management policies in Canada.

Tsilhqot'in Nation v. British Columbia (2014): As previously discussed, the Tsilhqot'in decision was a landmark case in recognizing Indigenous title over specific land areas. The Supreme Court's ruling confirmed the Tsilhqot'in Nation's claim to their traditional territory and established principles for asserting Aboriginal title.

Implications: The Tsilhqot'in decision marked a significant advancement in Indigenous land rights, providing a clear framework for recognizing and enforcing Aboriginal title. It underscored the need for meaningful consultation and consent in resource development and land management.

Kirkland Lake v. Eabametoong First Nation (2021): This recent case addressed issues of land use and resource extraction in relation to Indigenous rights. The Ontario Superior Court ruled in favor of the Eabametoong First Nation, affirming their rights to be consulted on developments impacting their traditional lands.

Implications: The Kirkland Lake decision reinforced the principles of consultation and accommodation, emphasizing the need for governments and industries to engage with Indigenous communities. It highlighted the ongoing challenges and complexities in balancing development with Indigenous land rights.

The Broader Impact of Court Decisions

Shaping Policies and Legislation: Court decisions have influenced federal and provincial policies and legislation related to Indigenous land rights. The recognition of Aboriginal title and the duty to consult have led to legislative reforms and the negotiation of land claims and treaties.

Promoting Reconciliation: Judicial rulings have played a role in advancing reconciliation efforts by acknowledging historical injustices and validating Indigenous rights. The recognition of Aboriginal title and the duty to consult are steps toward addressing past wrongs and fostering respectful relationships between Indigenous communities and the Crown.

Challenges and Limitations: Despite significant legal victories, Indigenous communities continue to face challenges in realizing their land rights. Implementation of court decisions can be slow, and governments may resist fully recognizing or respecting Indigenous rights. Ongoing advocacy and legal action are necessary to address these challenges and ensure that court rulings translate into meaningful change.

The Reserve System and Its Consequences

The Economic, Social, and Cultural Impact of the Reserve System on Indigenous Communities

The reserve system established in the late 19th and early 20th centuries has had profound and lasting effects on Indigenous communities across Canada. Initially designed to confine and control Indigenous peoples, the system has led to a range of economic, social, and cultural impacts. This section explores these impacts in detail, highlighting how the reserve system has shaped the lives of Indigenous peoples and the ongoing challenges they face.

Economic Impact

Limited Economic Opportunities: The reserve system restricted Indigenous peoples to small, often less fertile parcels of land, which significantly limited their ability to engage in traditional economic activities such as hunting, fishing, and agriculture. The land allocated for reserves was frequently unsuitable for productive use, hindering economic development and self-sufficiency.

Case Study: The Impact on Agriculture: Many reserves were situated on lands with poor soil quality, making agriculture difficult. For instance, reserves in the Prairie provinces were often located on less fertile land compared to the surrounding agricultural land. This limitation severely impacted the ability of Indigenous communities to engage in farming and other economic activities that could sustain their communities.

Economic Dependency on Government Assistance: The reserve system fostered a dependency on government assistance. With restricted land and limited resources, many Indigenous communities became reliant on federal support for basic necessities. This dependency has persisted, contributing to ongoing socio-economic challenges and disparities between Indigenous and non-Indigenous populations.

Case Study: The Indian Act and Economic Control: The Indian Act's restrictions on economic activities, such as limiting the ability to lease or sell reserve land, reinforced economic dependency. For example, the Act's control over land use and economic activities prevented many communities from engaging in resource development or other economic ventures that could have provided financial independence.

Challenges in Resource Development: The reserve system has also hindered the ability of Indigenous communities to capitalize on natural resources located on their lands. Despite the presence of valuable resources such as minerals and oil, reserve land often remains under the control of the federal government, limiting Indigenous communities' ability to benefit from these resources.

Case Study: Resource Development and Negotiations: In some cases, Indigenous communities have sought to negotiate resource development agreements. However, these negotiations are often complex and protracted, with communities facing challenges in asserting their rights and ensuring fair compensation. For example, the development of oil sands projects in Alberta has led to legal battles over land rights and resource revenues.

Social Impact

Disruption of Traditional Lifestyles: The reserve system disrupted traditional Indigenous lifestyles and community structures. Indigenous peoples were often forcibly removed from their ancestral lands and relocated to reserves, leading to the loss of traditional practices and social cohesion.

Case Study: Forced Relocation and Social Disruption: The relocation of Indigenous communities to reserves disrupted traditional social structures and practices. For instance, the forced relocation of the Inuit from their traditional territories to new settlements in the Arctic resulted in significant cultural and social disruption, impacting community cohesion and well-being.

Health and Social Services: The reserve system has also had an impact on health and social services in Indigenous communities. Often, reserves have faced inadequate infrastructure and limited access to essential services such as healthcare, education, and social support.

Case Study: Health Disparities on Reserves: Health outcomes on reserves frequently lag behind national averages. Limited access to healthcare facilities and services, coupled with socio-economic challenges, has contributed to health disparities among Indigenous populations. For example, communities in remote or isolated reserves often face barriers to accessing healthcare services, resulting in higher rates of chronic illness and lower life expectancy.

Impact on Education: The reserve system has also affected educational opportunities for Indigenous youth. The education system on reserves has historically been underfunded and lacked resources compared to mainstream educational institutions.

Case Study: Educational Inequities: Educational outcomes in many Indigenous communities are lower than national averages. The lack of adequate funding, resources, and culturally relevant curricula has contributed to educational disparities. For example, schools on reserves often face challenges in providing quality education and addressing the specific needs of Indigenous students.

Cultural Impact

Erosion of Cultural Practices: The reserve system has contributed to the erosion of Indigenous cultures and languages. The confinement to reserves, coupled with policies aimed at assimilating Indigenous peoples, led to the suppression of traditional cultural practices and languages.

Case Study: The Impact of Residential Schools: The residential school system, which was closely tied to the reserve system, had a devastating impact on Indigenous cultures. Children were forcibly removed from their families and communities, resulting in the loss of cultural knowledge and language. The legacy of residential schools continues to affect Indigenous communities today.

Cultural Resilience and Revitalization: Despite the challenges posed by the reserve system, many Indigenous communities have demonstrated remarkable resilience and efforts to revitalize their cultures. Initiatives to preserve languages, revive traditional practices, and strengthen cultural identity are ongoing.

Case Study: Language and Cultural Revitalization: Many Indigenous communities have launched programs to revitalize their languages and cultural practices. For example, language immersion schools and cultural programs are helping to preserve Indigenous languages and traditions. These efforts are crucial in reclaiming and maintaining cultural heritage.

Community Identity and Autonomy: The reserve system has impacted the sense of community identity and autonomy. Indigenous communities have often struggled with issues of governance and self-determination due to the constraints imposed by the reserve system and the Indian Act.

Case Study: Self-Government Agreements: In recent years, some Indigenous communities have negotiated self-government agreements that aim to enhance autonomy and control over their lands and resources. These agreements represent a step toward addressing the legacy of the reserve system and empowering communities to manage their own affairs.

The Ongoing Challenges Related to Reserve Land, Including Limited Ownership and Access to Resources

The reserve system in Canada, while historically significant, has left Indigenous communities grappling with a range of ongoing challenges related to land ownership and access to resources. These challenges are deeply rooted in the policies and practices established by colonial and federal governments, and they continue to impact the socio-economic and cultural well-being of Indigenous peoples. This section explores these challenges in detail, highlighting how they perpetuate inequality and hinder the progress of Indigenous communities.

Limited Land Ownership

Ownership Constraints: One of the most significant challenges faced by Indigenous communities is the limited ability to own and control reserve land. Reserve lands are considered federal property, and Indigenous communities do not have outright ownership of the land. Instead, the land is held in trust by the federal government, which retains ultimate control over its use and management.

Case Study: Land Trusts and Ownership Limitations: The federal government's control over reserve lands means that Indigenous communities often face barriers to exercising full control over their land. For instance, in many cases, communities cannot lease or sell reserve land without federal approval. This limitation hampers their ability to engage in economic development and restricts their opportunities for land-based projects.

Legal and Administrative Barriers: The legal and administrative framework governing reserve lands adds another layer of complexity. The Indian Act and other federal policies impose restrictions on how reserve lands can be used, and the process for obtaining approvals or making changes is often bureaucratic and cumbersome.

Case Study: The Indian Act's Restrictions: The Indian Act imposes several restrictions on reserve land use. For example, any development or lease agreements require approval from Indigenous Services Canada (ISC), leading to delays and complications. This bureaucratic red tape often frustrates efforts to develop land and secure economic opportunities.

Fragmented Land Holdings: Reserve lands are often fragmented and scattered, resulting in inefficient land management and limited economic viability. Fragmented land holdings can also lead to disputes and challenges in coordinating land use and development projects.

Case Study: Fragmentation in Urban Reserves: In urban areas, reserve lands are frequently fragmented and interspersed with non-reserve lands. This fragmentation can create difficulties in managing land use and accessing resources. For example, urban reserves may face challenges in developing infrastructure or engaging in commercial ventures due to their isolated or fragmented nature.

Access to Resources

Restricted Resource Development: The reserve system limits Indigenous communities' ability to access and benefit from natural resources on their lands. Despite the presence of valuable resources such as minerals, oil, and timber, reserve lands are often subject to federal control, which can restrict Indigenous communities' involvement in resource development.

Case Study: Resource Development in Northern Communities: In northern communities where valuable resources like oil and minerals are present, Indigenous communities often face challenges in negotiating fair agreements and securing benefits from resource extraction. For example, communities in the Northwest Territories have struggled with negotiating equitable resource revenue-sharing agreements with mining companies and the federal government.

Revenue Sharing and Compensation: Even when resource development occurs on reserve lands, revenue-sharing arrangements and compensation for Indigenous communities can be inadequate. Agreements negotiated between communities and resource developers often fall short of providing fair compensation and benefits.

Case Study: Revenue Sharing Disputes: The Gitxsan and Wet'suwet'en Nations in British Columbia have been involved in protracted legal battles over resource development and revenue sharing. Disputes over compensation and benefits from resource projects have highlighted the ongoing challenges faced by Indigenous communities in securing fair agreements.

Environmental Degradation: Resource development on or near reserve lands can lead to environmental degradation, impacting the health and well-being of Indigenous communities. Pollution, habitat destruction, and other environmental issues can undermine traditional practices and negatively affect community health.

Case Study: Impact of Oil Sands Development: The expansion of oil sands development in Alberta has had significant environmental impacts on nearby Indigenous communities. Pollution from oil sands operations has affected air and water quality, leading to health issues and environmental concerns among affected communities.

Social and Economic Consequences

Economic Disparities: The limitations on land ownership and resource access contribute to economic disparities between Indigenous and non-Indigenous communities. The inability to fully utilize land and resources hinders economic development and perpetuates poverty in many Indigenous communities.

Case Study: Economic Disparities in Remote Communities: Remote Indigenous communities often face higher levels of poverty and unemployment compared to non-Indigenous communities. Limited access to economic opportunities and resources contributes to these disparities, making it challenging for communities to achieve economic self-sufficiency.

Social Displacement: The reserve system has led to social displacement and fragmentation within Indigenous communities. Limited land and resources can exacerbate social issues, including overcrowding, inadequate housing, and lack of access to essential services.

Case Study: Housing Shortages on Reserves: Many Indigenous communities experience housing shortages and inadequate living conditions due to restricted land availability. Overcrowded and substandard housing on reserves contributes to social and health challenges within these communities.

Cultural Impacts: The challenges related to land ownership and resource access also have cultural implications. The disruption of traditional land use practices and the inability to fully control land and resources can undermine cultural practices and community cohesion.

Case Study: Disruption of Traditional Practices: The restriction of land access has impacted traditional practices such as hunting, fishing, and ceremonial activities. For example, communities in the Yukon have faced difficulties maintaining traditional hunting practices due to land restrictions and environmental changes.

Chapter 5: Indigenous Resilience and Resistance

The Rise of Indigenous Activism

The Emergence of Indigenous Movements Advocating for Land Rights and Sovereignty

The struggle for Indigenous land rights and sovereignty in Canada has seen a resurgence in recent decades, with numerous movements and organizations emerging to advocate for the recognition and reclamation of Indigenous lands. These movements reflect a growing awareness of historical injustices and a concerted effort to address longstanding grievances regarding land dispossession and cultural erosion. This section explores the rise of these Indigenous movements, their key achievements, and the ongoing challenges they face.

Historical Context and Rise of Indigenous Activism

Historical Injustices and the Catalyst for Activism: The historical injustices faced by Indigenous peoples in Canada, including land dispossession, cultural suppression, and systemic discrimination, have been major catalysts for the emergence of Indigenous activism. The legacy of colonial policies and practices, such as the Indian Act and residential schools, created a sense of urgency among Indigenous communities to address these wrongs and assert their rights.

Case Study: The Impact of Residential Schools: The legacy of residential schools, which aimed to assimilate Indigenous children and erase their cultures, has been a significant factor in the rise of Indigenous activism. The trauma and loss experienced by survivors and their families have galvanized movements seeking justice and reparations for these abuses.

The 1960s and 1970s: Early Indigenous Activism: The 1960s and 1970s marked the beginning of organized Indigenous activism in Canada. This period saw the formation of key organizations and the beginning of significant legal and political battles for Indigenous rights. The Red Power movement, inspired by the American Indian Movement (AIM) in the United States, played a crucial role in raising awareness about Indigenous issues and advocating for change.

Case Study: The Formation of the Native Council of Canada: In 1968, the Native Council of Canada (now known as the Congress of Aboriginal Peoples) was established to represent the interests of off-reserve Indigenous peoples. The Council became a prominent voice in advocating for land rights and policy reforms.

Key Movements and Organizations

The Assembly of First Nations (AFN): The Assembly of First Nations, established in 1982, is one of the most influential organizations advocating for Indigenous rights in Canada. The AFN represents First Nations communities across the country and plays a central role in advocating for land rights, self-governance, and policy changes at the federal level.

Case Study: The AFN's Role in the Oka Crisis: The 1990 Oka Crisis, a land dispute between the Mohawk community of Kanesatake and the Canadian government, highlighted the AFN's role in advocating for Indigenous rights. The crisis drew national and international attention to Indigenous land claims and led to increased support for the AFN's initiatives.

The Truth and Reconciliation Commission (TRC): The Truth and Reconciliation Commission, established in 2008, was tasked with documenting the experiences of survivors of residential schools and addressing the legacy of these institutions. The TRC's findings and recommendations have played a crucial role in shaping public discourse on Indigenous issues and advocating for justice and reconciliation.

Case Study: The TRC's Calls to Action: The TRC's Calls to Action, released in 2015, included recommendations for addressing the impact of residential schools and advancing Indigenous land rights. These calls have influenced policy changes and advocacy efforts across Canada.

Land Defenders and Sovereignty Movements: In recent years, grassroots movements and land defenders have emerged to challenge resource extraction projects and assert Indigenous sovereignty. These movements often focus on protecting traditional lands from development and advocating for the recognition of Indigenous self-determination.

Case Study: The Wet'suwet'en Land Defenders: The Wet'suwet'en Nation's opposition to the Coastal GasLink pipeline project has been a prominent example of contemporary Indigenous activism. The Wet'suwet'en land defenders have mobilized national and international support to challenge the project and assert their right to control their traditional territories.

Achievements and Progress

Legal Victories and Land Claims Settlements: Indigenous movements have achieved significant legal victories and land claims settlements over the years. Court rulings and negotiated agreements have recognized Indigenous land rights and led to the return of lands and resources to Indigenous communities.

Case Study: The Tsilhqot'in Nation Decision: The 2014 Supreme Court of Canada decision in favor of the Tsilhqot'in Nation was a landmark victory for Indigenous land rights. The court recognized the Tsilhqot'in's title to a large area of land in British Columbia, affirming their right to control and benefit from their traditional territories.

Policy Changes and Government Commitments: Indigenous activism has led to policy changes and government commitments aimed at addressing historical injustices and advancing Indigenous rights. These changes include initiatives to improve land management practices, support self-governance, and enhance economic opportunities for Indigenous communities.

Case Study: The Implementation of the UNDRIP: Canada's endorsement of the United Nations Declaration on the Rights of Indigenous Peoples (UNDRIP) in 2016 marked a significant step toward recognizing and respecting Indigenous rights. The implementation of UNDRIP principles has influenced policy reforms and increased support for Indigenous land claims.

Ongoing Challenges

Continued Discrimination and Systemic Barriers: Despite progress, Indigenous communities continue to face discrimination and systemic barriers that hinder their efforts to secure land rights and sovereignty. Racism, bureaucratic obstacles, and inadequate government support persist as significant challenges.

Case Study: Ongoing Legal Battles: Many Indigenous communities are still engaged in legal battles to assert their land rights and challenge unjust policies. The ongoing struggle for justice reflects the persistence of systemic barriers and the need for continued advocacy.

Resource Development and Environmental Impact: Indigenous movements often confront challenges related to resource development and environmental impact. The pressure to balance economic development with environmental protection and cultural preservation remains a complex and contentious issue.

Case Study: The Impact of Pipeline Projects: Resource development projects, such as pipeline construction, frequently lead to conflicts between Indigenous communities and governments or corporations. These conflicts highlight the ongoing struggle to protect traditional lands and maintain environmental stewardship.

Internal Division and Diversity of Perspectives: Indigenous communities are not monolithic, and there are diverse perspectives and priorities within and between communities. Internal divisions and differing views on land use and development can complicate efforts to present a unified front in advocacy.

Case Study: Diverse Perspectives on Resource Development: Within Indigenous communities, there are varying opinions on resource development projects. While some communities support development for economic reasons, others prioritize environmental protection and cultural preservation. Navigating these diverse perspectives is an ongoing challenge for Indigenous movements.

Case Studies of Successful Land Reclamation Efforts and Legal Victories

This section explores key case studies of successful land reclamation efforts and legal victories by Indigenous communities in Canada. These examples illustrate the power of perseverance, legal strategy, and collective action in reclaiming land and asserting sovereignty. Each case provides insights into the diverse approaches used by Indigenous peoples to challenge historical injustices and secure their land rights.

1. Tsilhqot'in Nation v. British Columbia (2014)

Background: The Tsilhqot'in Nation, located in British Columbia, fought a prolonged legal battle to establish their land rights. The case centered on the claim to a large area of land in the central interior of British Columbia, which the Tsilhqot'in argued was their traditional territory and had been used and occupied for generations.

Legal Battle: The Tsilhqot'in Nation's legal struggle began in the 1980s, with efforts to assert their rights to the land through negotiations and legal proceedings. The case reached the Supreme Court of Canada, which delivered a landmark decision in 2014.

Victory: The Supreme Court of Canada ruled in favor of the Tsilhqot'in Nation, recognizing their title to approximately 1,750 square kilometers of land. This decision was groundbreaking, as it was the first time the Court had granted title to Indigenous land outside of a specific treaty agreement.

Impact: The ruling confirmed the Tsilhqot'in Nation's right to control and benefit from their traditional territory. It set a precedent for Indigenous land claims across Canada, affirming the legal recognition of Indigenous land rights and influencing subsequent legal and policy developments.

2. The Nunavut Land Claims Agreement (1993)

Background: The Nunavut Land Claims Agreement was negotiated between the Inuit of Nunavut and the Canadian government, following decades of advocacy and negotiation. The agreement aimed to address land claims and establish a new territory with a significant degree of self-governance for the Inuit.

Negotiation and Agreement: The agreement was finalized in 1993 and was one of the most comprehensive land claims settlements in Canadian history. It provided the Inuit with ownership of approximately 355,000 square kilometers of land, representing 18% of the territory of Nunavut.

Victory: The Nunavut Land Claims Agreement established the Nunavut Territory, with the Inuit holding significant control over land and resources. It also included provisions for financial compensation and resource revenue sharing.

Impact: The agreement marked a significant milestone in the recognition of Indigenous rights in Canada. It empowered the Inuit to govern many aspects of public policy, including education, health care, and social services, and set a model for other land claims agreements.

3. The Innu Nation's Land Claims Settlement (2008)

Background: The Innu Nation in Labrador sought recognition and compensation for lands that were traditionally used and occupied but had been taken without consent. The legal battle centered on the impact of hydroelectric development on their traditional territory.

Legal Battle: The Innu Nation's legal battle involved negotiations and legal proceedings to address the impact of resource development on their lands. The case was part of a broader effort to secure land rights and compensation for historical injustices.

Victory: In 2008, the Innu Nation reached a historic land claims settlement with the Canadian government. The agreement included compensation for the impact of hydroelectric development, as well as recognition of Innu land rights.

Impact: The settlement provided the Innu Nation with financial compensation and formal recognition of their land rights. It also established mechanisms for consultation and accommodation regarding resource development, marking a significant step in addressing the impacts of historical injustices.

4. The Ktunaxa Nation and the Ski Resort Dispute (2017)

Background: The Ktunaxa Nation, located in British Columbia, contested the development of a ski resort on a site they considered sacred. The development was proposed for an area with cultural and spiritual significance to the Ktunaxa people.

Legal Battle: The Ktunaxa Nation challenged the development on the grounds that it violated their constitutional rights and traditional values. The case involved legal arguments related to Indigenous rights and the duty to consult and accommodate.

Victory: In 2017, the Supreme Court of Canada ruled in favor of the Ktunaxa Nation, recognizing their right to be consulted and accommodated in decisions affecting their traditional territories. While the ruling did not stop the development entirely, it affirmed the Ktunaxa Nation's right to have their concerns considered.

Impact: The decision highlighted the importance of meaningful consultation with Indigenous communities regarding resource development. It reinforced the duty of governments and developers to respect Indigenous rights and values in decision-making processes.

5. The Six Nations Land Reclamation at Caledonia (2006–ongoing)

Background: The Six Nations of the Grand River initiated a land reclamation effort in Caledonia, Ontario, to assert their rights to lands they claimed were illegally taken from them. The reclamation began in 2006 and involved occupying land to protest and demand the return of their traditional territory.

Legal and Political Struggle: The Six Nations faced significant legal and political challenges in their reclamation efforts. The occupation led to conflicts with local authorities and discussions with federal and provincial governments.

Victory: While the reclamation has not resulted in a complete resolution, it has raised awareness of Indigenous land issues and pressured governments to address land claims. The ongoing effort continues to highlight the need for meaningful negotiations and agreements.

Impact: The Caledonia reclamation has been instrumental in bringing attention to Indigenous land rights and the challenges faced by communities seeking justice. It has also influenced discussions around land claims and negotiations in Canada.

Treaty Negotiations and Land Claims Agreements

The Role of Modern Treaties and Land Claims Agreements in Addressing Historical Injustices

Modern treaties and land claims agreements play a crucial role in addressing historical injustices and redefining the relationship between Indigenous communities and the Canadian government. These agreements represent an attempt to rectify past wrongs, acknowledge Indigenous rights, and establish frameworks for coexistence and self-determination. Here's a detailed exploration of how these agreements work and their impact on rectifying historical injustices.

**1. Overview of Modern Treaties and Land Claims Agreements

Modern Treaties: Modern treaties, also known as comprehensive land claims agreements, are negotiated between Indigenous groups and the Canadian government to settle outstanding land claims. Unlike historic treaties, which were often signed under duress or through misunderstanding, modern treaties aim to address specific grievances and provide a clear framework for land rights and governance.

Land Claims Agreements: Land claims agreements are formal documents that outline the rights and obligations of parties involved in settling land disputes. These agreements typically cover land ownership,

resource management, and self-governance. They are intended to provide fair compensation and recognition of Indigenous rights while ensuring that future disputes are resolved through agreed-upon
mechanisms.

**2. Historical Context and Necessity

Addressing Historical Wrongs: Historical injustices, including land
dispossession, forced assimilation, and cultural suppression, have left
Indigenous communities with significant grievances. The legacy of colonial policies, such as the Indian Act and reserve system, has marginalized
Indigenous peoples and disrupted their traditional ways of life.

Necessity of Modern Agreements: Modern treaties and land claims
agreements are essential for addressing these historical wrongs. They offer a formal mechanism to recognize and rectify past injustices, provide
land and resource rights, and promote reconciliation. These agreements
represent a shift from unilateral decision-making to collaborative negotiation and partnership.

**3. Key Components of Modern Treaties and Land Claims Agree-
ments

Land and Resource Rights: One of the primary components of
modern treaties is the transfer of land and resource rights to Indigenous
communities. This often includes the return of traditional territories,
rights to natural resources, and financial compensation. These provisions aim to restore control over lands that were unjustly taken and to
support economic development.

Self-Governance: Modern treaties typically include provisions for
self-governance, allowing Indigenous communities to manage their
own affairs and make decisions that affect their lives. This includes control over education, health services, and other essential areas of governance. Self-governance empowers communities to preserve their
cultural practices and implement policies aligned with their values.

Consultation and Accommodation: Modern treaties emphasize the
importance of consultation and accommodation in decisions affecting
Indigenous lands and resources. This requirement ensures that Indige-

nous communities are involved in the planning and decision-making processes that impact their territories. It aims to prevent conflicts and ensure that Indigenous rights are respected.

**4. Impact of Modern Treaties and Land Claims Agreements

Recognition and Restoration: Modern treaties have led to the formal recognition of Indigenous land rights and the restoration of traditional territories. By providing legal recognition and compensation, these agreements help address the historical injustices of land dispossession and support the revival of Indigenous cultures and practices.

Economic Development: The transfer of land and resource rights through modern treaties has facilitated economic development within Indigenous communities. Access to natural resources and financial compensation enables communities to invest in infrastructure, education, and business ventures, contributing to long-term economic growth and self-sufficiency.

Empowerment and Self-Determination: Modern treaties and land claims agreements empower Indigenous communities by granting self-governance and decision-making authority. This empowerment enables communities to implement policies that reflect their values and priorities, fostering cultural preservation and community resilience.

**5. Challenges and Limitations

Implementation and Administration: Despite their importance, modern treaties face challenges in implementation and administration. Disputes over the interpretation of agreements, delays in fulfilling commitments, and bureaucratic obstacles can hinder progress. Ensuring effective implementation and administration is crucial for realizing the full benefits of these agreements.

Ongoing Disputes and Negotiations: Modern treaties do not always resolve all disputes or address every grievance. Ongoing negotiations and additional agreements may be required to address unresolved issues or emerging concerns. Continuous dialogue and negotiation are necessary to address evolving challenges and ensure that agreements remain relevant and effective.

Equity and Inclusivity: There are concerns about the inclusivity and equity of modern treaties. Some Indigenous communities may feel that agreements do not fully address their needs or that certain groups are marginalized. Ensuring that all voices are heard and that agreements reflect the diverse perspectives of Indigenous communities is essential for achieving true reconciliation.

**6. Case Studies of Modern Treaties and Land Claims Agreements

Nunavut Land Claims Agreement (1993): The Nunavut Land Claims Agreement was a landmark agreement that established the Nunavut Territory and provided the Inuit with significant land and resource rights. The agreement has been instrumental in promoting Inuit self-governance and economic development.

James Bay and Northern Quebec Agreement (1975): This agreement, signed with the Cree and Inuit of northern Quebec, marked the first comprehensive land claims agreement in Canada. It addressed land rights, resource management, and compensation, setting a precedent for future agreements.

Yukon Land Claims Settlements (1990s): The Yukon Land Claims Settlements resulted in agreements with various First Nations in Yukon, providing land rights, resource access, and self-governance. These agreements have supported economic development and cultural preservation in the region.

Analysis of Key Agreements: The Nunavut Land Claims Agreement and Its Impact on Indigenous Communities

The Nunavut Land Claims Agreement (NLCA) stands as a landmark in Canada's history of Indigenous relations, representing one of the most comprehensive land claims agreements ever made. This section analyzes the Nunavut Land Claims Agreement, exploring its significance, implementation, and the impact it has had on Indigenous communities, particularly the Inuit of Nunavut.

**1. Historical Context and Formation of the Nunavut Land Claims Agreement

Historical Background: Prior to the NLCA, the Inuit of the Eastern Arctic faced significant challenges related to land rights and self-determination. The lack of formal recognition for their traditional territories, coupled with the pressures of modernization and development, highlighted the need for a comprehensive land claims process.

Negotiation and Settlement: The Nunavut Land Claims Agreement was negotiated between the Inuit Tapiriit Kanatami (ITK), representing the Inuit of the Eastern Arctic, and the Government of Canada. The negotiations began in the 1970s and culminated in the signing of the NLCA in 1993. This agreement was a response to longstanding grievances and aimed to address historical injustices by providing the Inuit with a formal land claim settlement.

**2. Key Components of the Nunavut Land Claims Agreement

Land Ownership and Resource Rights: The NLCA granted the Inuit ownership of approximately 355,000 square kilometers of land, representing about 18% of the territory of Nunavut. This included both surface and subsurface rights, allowing the Inuit to manage and benefit from natural resources within their traditional territories. The agreement also provided financial compensation and access to royalties from resource development.

Governance and Self-Government: A significant aspect of the NLCA was the establishment of the Nunavut Territory, which was created in 1999 as a result of the agreement. The Nunavut government, established under the NLCA, has jurisdiction over many areas of public policy, including education, health care, and natural resources. This self-governance structure enables the Inuit to exercise greater control over their political and administrative affairs, aligning policies with their cultural values and needs.

Environmental Protection and Land Use: The NLCA includes provisions for environmental protection and sustainable land use. It established mechanisms for consultation and cooperation between the Inuit and the federal government regarding land and resource management. This ensures that development activities are conducted in a manner that respects Inuit cultural practices and environmental values.

**3. Impact on Indigenous Communities

Economic Development: The Nunavut Land Claims Agreement has facilitated economic development within the Inuit communities. Access to land and resource rights has allowed for investments in infrastructure, mining, and other economic activities. This has led to job creation, increased economic opportunities, and improved living standards in Nunavut.

Cultural Preservation and Revitalization: The agreement has played a crucial role in the preservation and revitalization of Inuit culture. By granting control over traditional territories, the NLCA has enabled the Inuit to practice and maintain their cultural traditions, including hunting, fishing, and land-based activities. This cultural preservation contributes to the overall well-being and identity of the Inuit communities.

Political Empowerment and Self-Determination: The establishment of the Nunavut Territory and the self-governance provisions under the NLCA have significantly empowered the Inuit politically. The ability to govern their own affairs and make decisions affecting their communities has fostered a sense of autonomy and self-determination. This political empowerment is essential for addressing local needs and addressing issues specific to Inuit communities.

Social and Health Improvements: The NLCA has also had a positive impact on social and health outcomes in Nunavut. With control over governance and public policy, the Nunavut government has implemented programs and services that are tailored to the unique needs of Inuit communities. This includes improvements in health care, education, and social services, contributing to overall quality of life.

**4. Challenges and Ongoing Issues

Implementation and Bureaucracy: Despite the positive impacts, there have been challenges related to the implementation of the NLCA. Issues such as bureaucratic delays, disagreements over resource management, and the complexities of negotiating and enforcing provisions have posed difficulties. Addressing these challenges is crucial for ensuring the full realization of the agreement's benefits.

Resource Development and Environmental Concerns: The development of natural resources in Nunavut has raised concerns about environmental impact and sustainability. Balancing economic development with environmental protection is an ongoing challenge. Ensuring that resource extraction activities are conducted responsibly and in accordance with Inuit values is essential for maintaining ecological integrity.

Equity and Inclusion: While the NLCA has made significant strides, there are concerns about equity and inclusion. Ensuring that all Inuit communities benefit equally from the agreement and addressing any disparities or marginalization within the region are important considerations for achieving comprehensive justice and reconciliation.

Economic Development and Land Stewardship

Indigenous-Led Initiatives for Sustainable Land Management and Economic Development

The quest for sustainable land management and economic development has become a central focus for many Indigenous communities in Canada. Embracing their traditional knowledge and values, these communities are leading innovative initiatives that blend environmental stewardship with economic growth. This section examines various Indigenous-led initiatives that highlight their commitment to sustainable land management and economic development.

**1. Traditional Ecological Knowledge (TEK) and Land Management

Traditional Ecological Knowledge: Indigenous peoples have long utilized Traditional Ecological Knowledge (TEK) to manage their lands sustainably. TEK encompasses a deep understanding of the environment, including ecological processes, species behavior, and seasonal patterns. This knowledge is passed down through generations and provides valuable insights into sustainable land management practices.

Application of TEK: Modern Indigenous-led initiatives often incorporate TEK to guide land management decisions. For example, Indigenous fire management practices, such as controlled burning, are employed to prevent larger wildfires and promote ecological health. By integrating TEK with contemporary scientific methods, Indigenous communities effectively manage their lands while preserving their cultural heritage.

Case Study - The Firesticks Alliance: The Firesticks Alliance, led by Aboriginal rangers in Australia, is a notable example of how Indigenous fire management practices can enhance land management. By using traditional burning techniques to reduce fuel loads and prevent larger fires, the Alliance has demonstrated the effectiveness of integrating TEK with modern fire management strategies.

**2. Community-Based Resource Management

Community-Led Resource Management: Many Indigenous communities have established community-based resource management systems that prioritize environmental sustainability and community well-being. These systems empower local communities to make decisions about resource use, conservation, and development.

Example - The Tla-o-qui-aht First Nation: The Tla-o-qui-aht First Nation in British Columbia has developed a community-based resource management plan that emphasizes sustainable forestry practices. By implementing rigorous environmental standards and involving community members in decision-making, the Tla-o-qui-aht First Nation has successfully managed their forest resources while ensuring ecological integrity and economic benefits for their community.

Example - The Taku River Tlingit First Nation: The Taku River Tlingit First Nation in Yukon has established a collaborative management framework for their traditional territories. By working with government agencies and industry partners, the Taku River Tlingit First Nation has secured a role in managing natural resources and ensuring that development aligns with their cultural values and environmental priorities.

**3. Indigenous-Led Economic Development Initiatives

Renewable Energy Projects: Indigenous communities are increasingly investing in renewable energy projects as a means of achieving economic independence and reducing reliance on fossil fuels. These projects align with environmental values and offer long-term economic benefits.

Example - The Kainai First Nation Solar Project: The Kainai First Nation in Alberta has launched a solar energy project that harnesses the power of the sun to generate electricity for their community. This initiative not only provides a sustainable energy source but also creates job opportunities and revenue for the Kainai First Nation.

Example - The Innu Nation's Hydro Project: The Innu Nation in Labrador has been involved in developing hydroelectric projects on their traditional lands. By partnering with industry and government, the Innu Nation is leveraging their land rights to gain economic benefits while contributing to the transition to renewable energy sources.

Eco-Tourism Ventures: Eco-tourism initiatives led by Indigenous communities offer a way to showcase their cultural heritage while promoting environmental conservation. These ventures create economic opportunities and foster greater appreciation for Indigenous knowledge and traditions.

Example - The Haida Gwaii Eco-Tourism Initiative: The Haida Nation in British Columbia has developed an eco-tourism initiative that highlights their cultural heritage and natural beauty. By offering guided tours, cultural experiences, and educational programs, the Haida Nation generates revenue and promotes sustainable tourism practices that benefit both the community and the environment.

**4. Legal and Policy Advocacy for Sustainable Development

Advocacy for Indigenous Rights: Indigenous-led initiatives often involve advocacy for legal and policy changes that support sustainable land management and economic development. By engaging with policymakers and legal institutions, Indigenous communities seek to ensure that their rights and interests are recognized and protected.

Example - The Assembly of First Nations (AFN): The Assembly of First Nations advocates for policies that support Indigenous land rights and sustainable development. Through lobbying efforts and legal challenges, the AFN aims to influence government policies and ensure that Indigenous communities have a voice in land management and economic decisions.

Example - The Indigenous Climate Action Network: The Indigenous Climate Action Network is a coalition of Indigenous organizations and activists working to address climate change and promote sustainable development. By advocating for climate justice and supporting Indigenous-led solutions, the network seeks to advance environmental and economic goals that align with Indigenous values.

**5. Challenges and Future Directions

Funding and Resources: One of the challenges faced by Indigenous-led initiatives is securing adequate funding and resources. Many projects rely on external grants and support, and ensuring sustainable funding is crucial for their long-term success.

Capacity Building: Building capacity within Indigenous communities is essential for the success of land management and economic development initiatives. Providing education, training, and technical support helps communities develop the skills and knowledge needed to implement and sustain their projects.

Collaboration and Partnerships: Collaborating with government agencies, industry partners, and non-governmental organizations can enhance the effectiveness of Indigenous-led initiatives. Building strong partnerships and fostering mutual respect are key to achieving shared goals and addressing common challenges.

The Potential for Resource Revenue Sharing and the Assertion of Mineral Rights

The assertion of mineral rights and the potential for resource revenue sharing represent critical avenues for advancing Indigenous economic interests and self-determination in Canada. Historically marginalized in resource development decisions, Indigenous communities are increasingly seeking to assert control over their traditional lands and benefit from the economic opportunities that resource extraction offers. This section explores the potential for resource revenue sharing, the assertion of mineral rights, and the implications for Indigenous communities.

**1. The Context of Mineral Rights and Resource Revenue Sharing

Historical Dispossession and Resource Extraction: Indigenous communities have long been excluded from decisions about resource extraction on their traditional lands. The historical dispossession of Indigenous lands has left many communities with limited control over the resources within their territories. The assertion of mineral rights and resource revenue sharing is a means of addressing these historical injustices and securing economic benefits for Indigenous peoples.

Resource Revenue Sharing: Resource revenue sharing involves the distribution of financial benefits derived from resource extraction, such as mining, oil, and gas, to Indigenous communities. This arrangement aims to provide Indigenous communities with a share of the revenues generated by resource development on their traditional lands.

Legal and Policy Framework: Resource revenue sharing agreements are often negotiated as part of broader land claims agreements, treaties, or impact benefit agreements (IBAs). These agreements outline the terms of revenue sharing, including the percentage of revenue allocated to Indigenous communities and the mechanisms for distributing funds.

**2. Case Studies of Resource Revenue Sharing

The Nisga'a Treaty: The Nisga'a Treaty, signed in 1998, was one of the first modern treaties in British Columbia. It includes provisions for resource revenue sharing, providing the Nisga'a Nation with a share of revenues from resource development within their traditional territory.

The treaty has served as a model for other agreements and demonstrates the potential for revenue sharing to benefit Indigenous communities.

The Sahtu Dene and Métis Land Claim Agreement: The Sahtu Dene and Métis Land Claim Agreement, signed in 1993, includes provisions for resource revenue sharing from mineral and oil and gas development. The agreement established a resource revenue fund that supports community development projects and economic initiatives. This case highlights the positive impact of revenue sharing on community well-being and economic development.

The Yukon First Nations Land Claims Agreements: Several Yukon First Nations have negotiated land claims agreements that include provisions for resource revenue sharing. These agreements provide First Nations with a share of revenues from mining and other resource developments. The revenue sharing arrangements support community infrastructure, social programs, and economic development projects.

**3. The Assertion of Mineral Rights

Legal Precedents and Land Claims: The assertion of mineral rights by Indigenous communities is often grounded in legal precedents established by court decisions and land claims agreements. These legal frameworks affirm the rights of Indigenous peoples to control and benefit from resources on their traditional lands.

The Tsilhqot'in Nation Case: The 2014 Supreme Court of Canada decision in Tsilhqot'in Nation v. British Columbia was a landmark case that granted the Tsilhqot'in Nation title to a significant portion of their traditional territory. This decision included recognition of the Tsilhqot'in's rights to the minerals and resources within their territory. The case set a precedent for asserting Indigenous mineral rights and has influenced subsequent legal and policy developments.

The Mikisew Cree First Nation Case: The Mikisew Cree First Nation has been involved in legal battles over their mineral rights and resource development on their traditional lands. The Nation's efforts to assert their rights have led to negotiations with government and industry partners to secure revenue sharing and benefit agreements.

The Fort McKay First Nation Case: The Fort McKay First Nation in Alberta has negotiated agreements with oil sands companies to secure revenue sharing and environmental protection measures. These agreements aim to balance resource development with the protection of traditional lands and cultural values.

**4. Implications for Indigenous Communities

Economic Empowerment: Resource revenue sharing and the assertion of mineral rights provide Indigenous communities with economic opportunities and financial resources to support community development and self-sufficiency. Revenue from resource development can be used to fund education, healthcare, infrastructure, and other essential services.

Self-Determination and Governance: Securing control over mineral rights and participating in revenue sharing agreements enhance Indigenous self-determination and governance. By having a stake in resource development, Indigenous communities can influence decision-making processes and ensure that development aligns with their values and priorities.

Environmental Stewardship: Resource revenue sharing agreements often include provisions for environmental protection and sustainable development practices. Indigenous communities play a crucial role in ensuring that resource extraction is conducted in an environmentally responsible manner, preserving their lands for future generations.

Challenges and Considerations: Despite the potential benefits, resource revenue sharing and the assertion of mineral rights present challenges. Negotiating agreements can be complex and time-consuming, and communities must navigate legal, regulatory, and industry landscapes. Ensuring that revenue sharing arrangements are fair and transparent is essential for building trust and achieving positive outcomes.

**5. Future Directions

Strengthening Legal Frameworks: Ongoing efforts to strengthen legal frameworks and policies related to Indigenous mineral rights and revenue sharing are crucial. Continued advocacy and legal action can help ensure that Indigenous rights are respected and that communities receive a fair share of the benefits from resource development.

Building Partnerships: Collaborating with government, industry, and non-governmental organizations can enhance the effectiveness of resource revenue sharing and mineral rights initiatives. Building strong partnerships based on mutual respect and shared goals can facilitate successful negotiations and implementation.

Supporting Capacity Building: Investing in capacity building and technical expertise within Indigenous communities is essential for managing resource revenue and asserting mineral rights. Providing training and support can help communities navigate complex agreements and maximize the benefits of resource development.

7

Chapter 6: The Way Forward: Reclaiming Indigenous

T he Way Forward: Reclaiming Indigenous Lands

Reimagining Land Ownership and Governance

Proposals for Reforming Land Ownership Laws to Empower Indigenous Communities

In the face of ongoing land dispossession and systemic marginalization, reforming land ownership laws to empower Indigenous communities is not just a matter of justice, but also a critical step towards reconciling historical wrongs and ensuring equitable development. This section outlines several proposals aimed at overhauling current land ownership frameworks, strengthening Indigenous land rights, and fostering a more inclusive and just system.

**1. Recognition of Indigenous Land Rights

Legal Reforms to Recognize Indigenous Title: One of the most pressing reforms needed is the legal recognition of Indigenous land titles. Current land ownership laws often fail to fully acknowledge the traditional land rights of Indigenous communities. Legislative changes should formalize recognition of Indigenous land claims and grant legal title to traditional territories.

Implementation of the United Nations Declaration on the Rights of Indigenous Peoples (UNDRIP): Adopting and implementing UN-

DRIP's principles can guide reforms in land ownership laws. This includes respecting Indigenous land rights, ensuring free, prior, and informed consent for land use decisions, and acknowledging Indigenous peoples' connection to their traditional lands.

**2. Empowering Indigenous Land Management

Transfer of Land Ownership to Indigenous Communities: Reforming land ownership laws should include mechanisms for transferring land ownership from federal and provincial governments to Indigenous communities. This would involve returning lands that were historically dispossessed, as well as granting title to lands that Indigenous communities currently occupy.

Support for Indigenous Land Trusts and Governance Structures: Establishing land trusts and governance structures managed by Indigenous communities can facilitate effective land management. These entities would be responsible for overseeing land use, development, and conservation in accordance with Indigenous values and traditions.

Capacity Building for Indigenous Land Management: Investing in capacity building for Indigenous communities is crucial. This includes providing training and resources to manage land effectively, develop land-use plans, and implement sustainable practices. Enhancing technical expertise and governance capabilities will empower communities to assert control over their lands.

**3. Revising the Indian Act and Reserve System

Abolition or Reform of the Indian Act: The Indian Act has been a significant barrier to Indigenous land ownership and self-governance. Reforming or abolishing the Act and replacing it with legislation that supports self-determination and Indigenous land rights is essential. New laws should address land ownership, governance, and the protection of Indigenous cultural practices.

Expansion of Self-Government Agreements: Expanding self-government agreements can provide Indigenous communities with greater control over their lands and resources. These agreements should include provisions for land ownership, management, and decision-making authority.

Review and Reform of the Reserve System: The reserve system has historically marginalized Indigenous communities by confining them to small, often unsuitable parcels of land. Reforming the reserve system to allow for more flexible land use and management, and providing opportunities for land expansion, can help address some of the limitations imposed by this system.

**4. Strengthening Land Claims Processes

Streamlining Land Claims Negotiations: The current land claims process can be lengthy and complex, often resulting in delays and dissatisfaction. Reforming the process to make it more efficient, transparent, and equitable can help expedite the resolution of land claims and ensure that Indigenous communities receive fair compensation and land returns.

Enhancing Support for Land Claims: Providing additional support and resources for Indigenous communities pursuing land claims is crucial. This includes funding for legal representation, research, and negotiation support to ensure that communities can effectively advocate for their rights.

Implementing Binding Agreements: Ensuring that land claims agreements are legally binding and enforceable is essential for upholding Indigenous land rights. This includes clear provisions for the return of lands, financial compensation, and the protection of cultural and environmental values.

**5. Promoting Economic Development and Revenue Sharing

Equitable Resource Revenue Sharing: Reforming land ownership laws should include provisions for equitable resource revenue sharing. Indigenous communities should receive a fair share of revenues from resource extraction activities on their traditional lands, with agreements that are transparent and beneficial to the community.

Support for Indigenous Economic Initiatives: Investing in Indigenous-led economic initiatives, including land-based enterprises and sustainable development projects, can help communities leverage their land rights for economic growth. Support for entrepreneurship, training, and infrastructure development is vital for fostering economic resilience.

Integration of Traditional Knowledge and Practices: Incorporating traditional knowledge and practices into land management and economic development can enhance sustainability and cultural preservation. Legal reforms should recognize and support the integration of Indigenous knowledge systems in land use planning and resource management.

**6. Addressing Environmental and Cultural Concerns

Strengthening Environmental Protections: Reforming land ownership laws should include provisions for robust environmental protections. Indigenous communities often have deep connections to their lands and natural resources, and ensuring that land management practices respect these connections is essential for preserving ecosystems and cultural heritage.

Cultural Preservation and Restoration: Legal reforms should also address the preservation and restoration of Indigenous cultural sites and practices. This includes protecting sacred sites, traditional hunting and fishing areas, and other cultural resources from development and exploitation.

Public Education and Awareness: Raising public awareness about Indigenous land rights and the historical context of dispossession is crucial for fostering support for reform efforts. Educational initiatives can help build understanding and empathy, paving the way for more effective and just policy changes.

The Potential Role of Indigenous Governance Structures in Managing Land and Resources

Indigenous governance structures offer a vital opportunity for managing land and resources in a manner that honors traditional knowledge, respects cultural values, and ensures sustainable stewardship.

These structures, rooted in millennia of Indigenous practices and insights, have the potential to transform land management in Canada, promoting a more equitable and effective system. This section explores the potential roles and benefits of Indigenous governance structures in managing land and resources, emphasizing how they can address historical injustices and contribute to a more balanced and inclusive approach.

**1. Traditional Knowledge and Stewardship Practices

Integration of Traditional Ecological Knowledge (TEK): Indigenous governance structures are uniquely positioned to integrate Traditional Ecological Knowledge (TEK) into land and resource management. TEK encompasses a deep understanding of ecosystems, species, and environmental processes developed over generations. By incorporating TEK, Indigenous governance can enhance environmental conservation, improve resource management, and address ecological challenges in ways that align with traditional practices.

Holistic Land Management Approaches: Indigenous governance often emphasizes a holistic approach to land management, which considers the interconnectedness of land, water, wildlife, and human activities. This approach contrasts with conventional methods that may focus narrowly on resource extraction or economic gains. By prioritizing the health of entire ecosystems, Indigenous governance structures can promote long-term sustainability and resilience.

**2. Self-Governance and Autonomy

Empowerment Through Self-Governance: Indigenous governance structures provide a framework for self-governance, empowering communities to make decisions about their lands and resources. This autonomy allows communities to develop and implement policies that reflect their values, priorities, and traditional practices. Self-governance ensures that decisions about land use, conservation, and development are made by those who are directly affected and have a vested interest in maintaining the land's health and cultural significance.

Local Decision-Making and Accountability: Indigenous governance structures often operate at the local level, enabling more responsive and accountable decision-making. Unlike centralized or bureaucratic systems, local governance structures can address issues promptly and adapt policies to meet specific community needs. This localized approach fosters greater engagement and accountability, ensuring that land and resource management aligns with community goals.

**3. Economic Development and Resource Management

Community-Led Economic Initiatives: Indigenous governance structures can drive community-led economic initiatives that capitalize on local resources and traditional knowledge. By managing resources and overseeing development projects, Indigenous communities can create economic opportunities that benefit their members and support cultural preservation. For example, communities can develop sustainable tourism, eco-friendly industries, or renewable energy projects that align with their values.

Resource Revenue Sharing and Management: Effective resource management under Indigenous governance can also involve equitable revenue sharing arrangements. Indigenous communities should have a fair share of revenues from resource extraction activities on their traditional lands. This approach ensures that economic benefits from resource development contribute to community well-being and support investments in education, health, and infrastructure.

**4. Legal and Institutional Frameworks

Development of Indigenous Land Trusts: Establishing Indigenous land trusts can provide a formal mechanism for managing land and resources. These trusts can be structured to hold title to land, oversee land use, and ensure that resources are managed according to community-defined principles. Land trusts can also facilitate partnerships with government and private sector entities while maintaining community control over key decisions.

Negotiating Modern Treaties and Agreements: Indigenous governance structures play a crucial role in negotiating modern treaties and land claims agreements. These agreements can establish clear terms for land ownership, resource management, and economic benefits. Indigenous governance ensures that these negotiations reflect community interests and priorities, leading to agreements that provide lasting benefits and protect cultural values.

**5. Cultural and Environmental Preservation

Protection of Sacred Sites and Cultural Heritage: Indigenous governance structures are essential for protecting sacred sites and cultural heritage. These structures can establish protocols and safeguards to prevent desecration or exploitation of culturally significant areas. By integrating cultural considerations into land management, Indigenous governance ensures that traditional practices and spiritual connections are honored and preserved.

Sustainable Resource Management Practices: Sustainability is a core principle in many Indigenous governance systems. By implementing sustainable resource management practices, Indigenous governance can help mitigate environmental degradation and promote ecological balance. This includes practices such as controlled hunting, sustainable forestry, and conservation efforts that align with traditional ecological knowledge.

**6. Challenges and Opportunities

Navigating Legal and Regulatory Barriers: Despite the potential benefits, Indigenous governance structures may face legal and regulatory barriers that limit their effectiveness. These barriers can include conflicts with existing laws, lack of recognition for Indigenous rights, and challenges in negotiating with government and industry stakeholders. Addressing these barriers requires ongoing advocacy, legal reform, and collaboration between Indigenous communities and external entities.

Building Capacity and Resources: To effectively manage land and resources, Indigenous governance structures need adequate resources and capacity. This includes funding for governance activities, training for community members, and support for developing management plans.

Investing in capacity building is essential for empowering Indigenous communities to fully realize their governance potential.

Policy Recommendations for Governments and Institutions

Recommendations for Federal and Provincial Governments to Support Indigenous Land Rights

To address the longstanding issues surrounding Indigenous land rights and to promote genuine reconciliation, federal and provincial governments in Canada must take substantive and proactive measures. This involves not only acknowledging historical wrongs but also implementing policies and practices that support Indigenous sovereignty, land stewardship, and economic development. The following recommendations outline critical steps that governments should take to support Indigenous land rights effectively:

**1. Acknowledge and Rectify Historical Injustices

Formal Apologies and Recognition: Governments should offer formal apologies for historical injustices related to land dispossession and displacement of Indigenous peoples. This includes acknowledging the systemic discrimination and violations of rights that have occurred. Public recognition and apology are crucial steps toward rebuilding trust and demonstrating a commitment to addressing past wrongs.

Comprehensive Land Restitution: Governments need to engage in comprehensive land restitution efforts to return land to Indigenous communities. This involves not only recognizing historical land claims but also actively working to transfer land titles and resources back to Indigenous ownership. Restitution should be guided by principles of justice, fairness, and respect for Indigenous rights.

**2. Enhance Legal and Policy Frameworks

Modernize Land Rights Legislation: Federal and provincial governments should modernize land rights legislation to better reflect Indigenous rights and aspirations. This includes updating laws to recognize

Indigenous land ownership, management, and governance structures. Legislation should support Indigenous self-determination and ensure that communities have the authority to make decisions about their lands and resources.

Strengthen the Implementation of Treaties: Governments must fulfill their obligations under existing treaties and land claims agreements. This involves honoring treaty terms, providing adequate compensation, and ensuring that agreements are implemented effectively. Governments should also engage in meaningful consultations with Indigenous communities to address any issues or disputes related to treaty implementation.

**3. Support Indigenous Land Management and Governance

Empower Indigenous Land Management Entities: Governments should support the establishment and capacity-building of Indigenous land management entities. This includes providing funding, resources, and technical assistance to Indigenous organizations that oversee land use, conservation, and development. Empowering these entities enhances Indigenous control and ensures that land management aligns with community values and priorities.

Promote Indigenous Governance Structures: Recognize and support Indigenous governance structures that reflect traditional practices and contemporary needs. This includes formalizing Indigenous governance systems, such as land trusts or councils, and ensuring they have the authority and resources needed to manage land and resources effectively. Governments should work collaboratively with Indigenous leaders to develop and implement governance frameworks.

**4. Facilitate Economic Development and Resource Revenue Sharing

Implement Resource Revenue Sharing Agreements: Governments should negotiate and implement resource revenue sharing agreements with Indigenous communities. These agreements ensure that communities receive a fair share of revenues from resource development activities on their traditional lands. Revenue sharing can support community development, infrastructure, and social programs, contributing to overall well-being.

Support Indigenous Economic Initiatives: Encourage and invest in Indigenous-led economic initiatives that leverage local resources and traditional knowledge. This includes supporting ventures in sustainable tourism, renewable energy, and other industries that align with Indigenous values and priorities. Providing financial assistance, training, and access to markets can help Indigenous businesses thrive and contribute to economic self-sufficiency.

**5. Ensure Meaningful Consultation and Participation

Strengthen Consultation Processes: Governments must ensure that consultation processes with Indigenous communities are meaningful and respectful. This involves engaging communities early in decision-making processes, providing clear and transparent information, and addressing concerns and feedback. Effective consultation ensures that Indigenous perspectives are incorporated into policy and project decisions.

Support Indigenous Participation in Policy Development: Encourage and facilitate Indigenous participation in the development of land and resource policies. This includes involving Indigenous representatives in policy discussions, advisory committees, and decision-making bodies. Ensuring that Indigenous voices are heard and valued in policy development leads to more inclusive and equitable outcomes.

**6. Invest in Education and Capacity Building

Fund Indigenous Education and Training Programs: Invest in education and training programs that build capacity within Indigenous communities. This includes supporting educational initiatives related to land management, governance, and resource development. Providing opportunities for skill development and knowledge acquisition empowers Indigenous individuals and strengthens community leadership.

Promote Research and Knowledge Sharing: Support research initiatives that explore Indigenous land management practices, cultural heritage, and resource management. Governments should collaborate with

Indigenous scholars, researchers, and communities to advance knowledge and share best practices. Research and knowledge sharing contribute to informed decision-making and effective land management.

**7. Address Environmental and Social Challenges

Enhance Environmental Protections: Governments should strengthen environmental protections to safeguard Indigenous lands and resources. This includes implementing regulations that prevent environmental degradation, support sustainable practices, and address climate change impacts. Collaborating with Indigenous communities on environmental stewardship can enhance conservation efforts and protect cultural and ecological values.

Provide Support for Social and Health Services: Ensure that Indigenous communities have access to adequate social and health services. This includes addressing issues such as inadequate housing, clean drinking water, and health care disparities. Supporting social and health services is essential for improving quality of life and ensuring that communities can fully participate in land and resource management.

**8. Foster Collaboration and Partnerships

Build Collaborative Relationships: Foster collaborative relationships between federal, provincial, and Indigenous governments. This involves working together on land management, policy development, and economic initiatives. Collaborative approaches ensure that solutions are mutually beneficial and address the needs and aspirations of Indigenous communities.

Encourage Public Awareness and Education: Promote public awareness and education about Indigenous land rights and historical injustices. Governments should support initiatives that educate Canadians about Indigenous history, culture, and contributions. Increasing public understanding fosters empathy, supports reconciliation efforts, and builds a foundation for respectful and informed policy-making.

The Importance of Consultation, Consent, and Collaboration in Land and Resource Decisions

In the context of Indigenous land and resource rights, the principles of consultation, consent, and collaboration are not just procedural requirements but fundamental components of justice and equity. These principles ensure that Indigenous communities have a meaningful role in decisions affecting their lands and resources, and they are crucial for addressing historical injustices and fostering respectful relationships. This section explores why these principles are vital, how they should be implemented, and the impacts they have on achieving fair and equitable outcomes.

1. The Principle of Consultation

Definition and Importance: Consultation is the process by which governments, corporations, and other entities engage with Indigenous communities to seek their input and feedback on proposed land and resource projects. This process is essential for acknowledging Indigenous rights and perspectives, particularly in contexts where projects may affect their traditional territories, cultural heritage, or ways of life.

Legal and Ethical Obligations: In Canada, the duty to consult Indigenous peoples is rooted in constitutional and legal obligations. The Supreme Court of Canada has established that governments must consult with Indigenous communities before making decisions that could impact their rights or interests. This duty is grounded in the recognition of Indigenous rights as well as international human rights standards.

Best Practices for Effective Consultation:

Early Engagement: Consultation should occur at the earliest stages of project planning and decision-making, ensuring that Indigenous communities have sufficient time to review and respond to proposals.

Transparent Processes: All information relevant to the project, including potential impacts and benefits, should be shared openly with Indigenous communities.

Respectful Dialogue: Consultation must be conducted in a manner that respects Indigenous cultures, traditions, and governance systems. This involves listening to and valuing Indigenous perspectives and addressing their concerns sincerely.

2. The Principle of Free, Prior, and Informed Consent (FPIC)

Definition and Significance: Free, Prior, and Informed Consent (FPIC) is a principle that requires obtaining explicit permission from Indigenous communities before proceeding with projects that affect their lands and resources. This principle goes beyond consultation to ensure that Indigenous peoples have full control over decisions impacting their traditional territories.

Legal Framework and International Standards: FPIC is recognized in various international agreements and declarations, including the United Nations Declaration on the Rights of Indigenous Peoples (UNDRIP). The principle underscores that Indigenous peoples have the right to determine their own development paths and to consent to or reject projects based on their own values and interests.

Implementing FPIC:

Free: Consent must be given voluntarily and without coercion or pressure. Indigenous communities should be able to make decisions based on their own free will, without external influence.

Prior: Consent should be obtained before any project activities begin. This ensures that Indigenous communities have a say in the planning and decision-making processes.

Informed: Indigenous communities must receive comprehensive and understandable information about the project, including potential risks, benefits, and alternatives, to make an informed decision.

3. The Principle of Collaboration

Definition and Importance: Collaboration involves working together with Indigenous communities in a cooperative and respectful manner to achieve shared goals and outcomes. This principle emphasizes the need for ongoing partnership and engagement rather than a one-time consultation or consent process.

Benefits of Collaboration:

Enhanced Decision-Making: Collaborative approaches lead to more informed and balanced decisions by integrating Indigenous knowledge, perspectives, and expertise into the process.

Mutual Benefits: Collaboration fosters relationships built on trust and respect, leading to mutually beneficial outcomes for both Indigenous communities and project proponents.

Conflict Resolution: Collaborative processes help to identify and address potential conflicts or concerns early, reducing the likelihood of disputes and fostering harmonious relationships.

Effective Collaborative Practices:

Building Relationships: Establishing strong, respectful relationships with Indigenous communities is crucial for successful collaboration. This involves recognizing and valuing Indigenous leadership and contributions.

Shared Goals: Collaborative efforts should focus on identifying and achieving shared goals and interests. This requires open communication and negotiation to find common ground.

Joint Planning and Implementation: Indigenous communities should be actively involved in all stages of project planning and implementation, from initial discussions to monitoring and evaluation.

4. Challenges and Obstacles

Institutional Barriers: Despite legal obligations and best practices, challenges often arise in the implementation of consultation, consent, and collaboration. These can include institutional resistance, inadequate resources, and insufficient commitment to meaningful engagement.

Community Capacity: Indigenous communities may face barriers related to capacity and resources when participating in consultation and collaboration processes. Ensuring that communities have the support and resources needed to effectively engage in these processes is essential for meaningful participation.

Power Imbalances: Power imbalances between Indigenous communities and project proponents can affect the fairness and effectiveness of consultation and collaboration. Addressing these imbalances requires acknowledging and addressing the inherent inequalities in decision-making processes.

5. Case Studies and Examples

Successful Consultation and Consent:

The Trans Mountain Pipeline Expansion: In this case, the consultation process with affected Indigenous communities was criticized for being inadequate, highlighting the need for more meaningful engagement and respect for FPIC principles. Lessons learned from this situation underscore the importance of thorough and respectful consultation processes.

Collaborative Land Management Initiatives:

The Joint Management of Protected Areas: Collaborative management agreements, such as those in national parks and protected areas, demonstrate how Indigenous knowledge and governance can enhance land stewardship and conservation efforts. These agreements often involve joint decision-making and shared responsibilities between Indigenous communities and government agencies.

Pathways to Reconciliation and Justice

The Role of Land Restitution in the Broader Context of Reconciliation Between Indigenous and Non-Indigenous Canadians

Land restitution is a pivotal component of reconciliation between Indigenous and non-Indigenous Canadians, representing both a symbolic gesture and a practical solution to address historical injustices. This process involves returning lands to Indigenous peoples, recognizing their inherent rights to their traditional territories, and rectifying the wrongs of past dispossession. Understanding the role of land restitution in reconciliation requires exploring its significance, challenges, and the broader implications for Canadian society.

1. Historical Context and Significance of Land Restitution

Historical Injustices: The history of land dispossession in Canada is marked by a series of policies and practices that systematically removed

Indigenous peoples from their ancestral lands. From early European settlements to the establishment of reserves and the imposition of the Indian Act, Indigenous communities have faced extensive land loss and marginalization. Land restitution seeks to address these historical injustices by returning control of lands to Indigenous peoples and acknowledging their rights to self-determination.

Symbolic Importance: Land restitution carries profound symbolic significance, representing a recognition of the inherent rights and sovereignty of Indigenous peoples. It is a powerful statement of respect and acknowledgment of past wrongs. Restoring land is not just about physical territory but also about restoring dignity, cultural heritage, and historical continuity.

Legal and Moral Imperatives: The legal and moral imperatives for land restitution are rooted in both Canadian law and international human rights standards. The Canadian constitution recognizes the rights of Indigenous peoples, and international frameworks such as the United Nations Declaration on the Rights of Indigenous Peoples (UNDRIP) affirm the rights to land and self-determination. Land restitution aligns with these principles by addressing the inequities imposed by historical and ongoing practices of dispossession.

2. The Process of Land Restitution

Negotiation and Agreements: Land restitution typically involves negotiations between Indigenous communities and governments or other entities responsible for the land. These negotiations can result in formal agreements that outline the terms of restitution, including the return of land, compensation, and conditions for management and stewardship. Successful negotiations require a commitment to meaningful engagement and a willingness to address the complexities of historical grievances.

Challenges and Obstacles: The process of land restitution can be fraught with challenges, including legal disputes, bureaucratic hurdles, and resistance from various stakeholders. Issues such as land title disputes, conflicting interests, and the need for comprehensive historical research can complicate restitution efforts. Overcoming these challenges requires a collaborative approach, transparency, and a focus on addressing the underlying issues that have led to land loss.

Successful Examples: Several successful examples of land restitution demonstrate the potential for positive outcomes when Indigenous communities and governments work together. For instance, the Nunavut Land Claims Agreement, which transferred significant land and resource rights to the Inuit, has been a model for reconciliation and self-determination. Similarly, the settlement of specific land claims, such as those involving the Haida Nation, has led to the return of traditional territories and the establishment of collaborative management frameworks.

3. Land Restitution and Reconciliation

Restoring Trust and Relationships: Land restitution plays a critical role in restoring trust and repairing relationships between Indigenous and non-Indigenous Canadians. By acknowledging and addressing past wrongs, land restitution fosters a sense of justice and respect. It creates opportunities for dialogue and collaboration, contributing to a more equitable and inclusive society.

Promoting Economic and Cultural Revitalization: The return of land can lead to significant economic and cultural revitalization for Indigenous communities. Land restitution provides the foundation for economic development, self-sufficiency, and cultural preservation. Access to traditional territories allows for the continuation of cultural practices, such as hunting, fishing, and land-based education, which are integral to Indigenous identity and well-being.

Broader Societal Implications: Land restitution has broader implications for Canadian society as a whole. It challenges the status quo of land ownership and usage, prompting a reevaluation of historical narratives and legal frameworks. It also promotes greater awareness and understanding of Indigenous issues among non-Indigenous Canadians, fostering a more informed and engaged public.

4. Moving Forward with Land Restitution

Strengthening Legal Frameworks: To support effective land restitution, there is a need for stronger legal frameworks that facilitate the return of land and resources to Indigenous communities. This includes reforms to existing laws and policies, as well as the development of new mechanisms that address the complexities of land restitution and ensure equitable outcomes.

Enhancing Collaboration and Support: Successful land restitution requires ongoing collaboration and support from all stakeholders, including government agencies, Indigenous organizations, and non-governmental organizations. Building partnerships and investing in capacity-building initiatives are essential for overcoming challenges and achieving sustainable outcomes.

Ensuring Accountability and Transparency: Accountability and transparency are crucial for maintaining trust and ensuring that land restitution processes are fair and effective. This involves clear communication, regular reporting, and mechanisms for addressing grievances and resolving disputes.

Fostering Education and Awareness: Education and awareness-raising efforts are vital for promoting understanding of land restitution and reconciliation issues. Engaging the broader public in discussions about the significance of land restitution and its role in reconciliation can help build support and create a more inclusive and informed society.

Strategies for Building a More Equitable and Just Future for All Canadians

Achieving a more equitable and just future for all Canadians involves addressing historical injustices, creating opportunities for all communities, and fostering inclusive policies that promote fairness and respect. Here are several strategies that can contribute to building a future where all Canadians can thrive:

1. Acknowledgment and Redress of Historical Injustices

Recognizing Past Wrongs: A crucial first step towards equity is the acknowledgment of historical injustices inflicted on Indigenous peoples and other marginalized groups. Governments, institutions, and individuals must confront and take responsibility for past wrongs, including land dispossession, cultural suppression, and systemic discrimination. Public acknowledgments, formal apologies, and educational initiatives can help foster understanding and reconciliation.

Compensation and Restitution: Implementing fair compensation mechanisms and restitution processes is essential for addressing historical wrongs. This includes the return of land, financial compensation, and support for rebuilding cultural and economic foundations. Ensuring that restitution efforts are comprehensive, transparent, and effectively address the needs of affected communities is key to achieving justice.

2. Strengthening Indigenous Rights and Self-Determination

Supporting Land Rights: Enhancing Indigenous land rights through modern treaties, land claims agreements, and legal recognition of traditional territories is vital for self-determination. Governments should prioritize negotiations with Indigenous communities to resolve land disputes and implement agreements that respect Indigenous sovereignty and governance.

Empowering Indigenous Governance: Strengthening Indigenous governance structures and supporting self-governance initiatives can empower communities to manage their own affairs and resources. This includes providing the necessary resources, training, and autonomy to Indigenous governments to effectively oversee land management, economic development, and social services.

Promoting Cultural Preservation: Investing in programs and initiatives that support the preservation and revitalization of Indigenous cultures, languages, and traditions is essential for cultural continuity and empowerment. Education programs, cultural centers, and community-led projects can play a significant role in maintaining and celebrating Indigenous heritage.

3. Addressing Systemic Inequities

Equitable Access to Services: Ensuring equitable access to essential services such as healthcare, education, and housing is fundamental for addressing systemic inequities. Governments and organizations should work to eliminate disparities in service delivery and invest in programs that address the unique needs of marginalized communities.

Economic Opportunities: Creating economic opportunities and reducing barriers to economic participation for disadvantaged groups can contribute to greater equity. This includes supporting small businesses, providing job training and education programs, and addressing barriers to employment. Economic development initiatives should be inclusive and designed to benefit all communities.

Equity in Policy Development: Incorporating equity considerations into policy development and decision-making processes is essential for creating fair and inclusive policies. This involves engaging diverse voices, conducting impact assessments, and ensuring that policies are designed to address the needs of all communities, particularly those that have been historically marginalized.

4. Fostering Inclusive Dialogue and Collaboration

Promoting Intercultural Understanding: Encouraging dialogue and understanding between different cultural groups can help build mutual respect and collaboration. Intercultural initiatives, community events, and educational programs can foster positive relationships and reduce prejudice.

Collaborative Governance: Adopting collaborative governance models that involve diverse stakeholders, including Indigenous communities, in decision-making processes can lead to more equitable outcomes. This includes establishing partnerships and advisory bodies that ensure all voices are heard and considered in policy development and implementation.

Building Public Awareness: Raising awareness about issues of equity and justice through public campaigns, media, and education can help create a more informed and empathetic society. Promoting understanding of historical contexts, current challenges, and potential solutions can mobilize support for equitable policies and initiatives.

5. Ensuring Accountability and Transparency

Monitoring and Reporting: Establishing mechanisms for monitoring and reporting on progress towards equity goals is crucial for accountability. This includes tracking the implementation of policies, measuring outcomes, and providing regular updates to the public and affected communities.

Addressing Complaints and Grievances: Creating accessible channels for individuals and communities to voice complaints and grievances ensures that issues are addressed in a timely and fair manner. Transparent processes for handling complaints and disputes can help build trust and ensure that all voices are heard.

Evaluating Impact: Regularly evaluating the impact of policies and initiatives on marginalized communities is essential for ensuring that they achieve their intended goals. Impact assessments and feedback mechanisms can provide valuable insights for improving and refining strategies.

6. Investing in Future Generations

Education and Empowerment: Investing in education and empowerment programs for young people from all backgrounds can create opportunities for future success. This includes providing access to quality education, mentorship, and leadership development programs that equip young people with the skills and confidence to contribute to their communities and society.

Supporting Innovation and Research: Encouraging innovation and research that addresses social, economic, and environmental challenges can drive progress towards a more equitable future. Supporting research initiatives that focus on the needs and experiences of marginalized communities can lead to the development of effective solutions and policies.

Building Resilient Communities: Strengthening community resilience through capacity-building, support networks, and infrastructure investments can help communities adapt to changes and thrive.

Resilient communities are better equipped to address challenges, seize
opportunities, and contribute to a more equitable society.

8

Conclusion

R eflections on the Struggle for Land and Justice

Summarizing the Historical and Ongoing Challenges Faced by Indigenous Communities in Reclaiming Their Lands

The journey of Indigenous communities in Canada to reclaim their ancestral lands is marked by a complex interplay of historical injustices and ongoing systemic challenges. The struggle for land rights reflects broader themes of dispossession, cultural erosion, and resistance against colonial and governmental frameworks. Here's a summary of the key historical and contemporary challenges faced by Indigenous communities in their pursuit of land reclamation.

Historical Dispossession and Land Grabs

Colonial Encroachment: From the moment European settlers arrived on the shores of North America, Indigenous lands were systematically appropriated. Early interactions between Indigenous peoples and European settlers were marked by the imposition of foreign legal and land ownership systems that disregarded Indigenous land stewardship and sovereignty. The seigneurial system in New France and subsequent British land grants laid the foundation for widespread dispossession.

Treaties and Agreements: The signing of treaties between Indigenous nations and colonial governments was a critical but flawed aspect of early land transactions. Many treaties were signed under duress, with significant power imbalances and limited understanding of the long-term implications. Treaties were often breached or misunderstood, lead-

| 143 |

ing to further loss of land and rights. The Royal Proclamation of 1763, intended to protect Indigenous lands, was frequently violated by settlers and government actions, undermining its effectiveness.

Legislative Measures: The establishment of the Indian Act in 1876 introduced a restrictive legal framework that further marginalized Indigenous peoples. This legislation controlled virtually every aspect of Indigenous life, from governance to land management. The creation of reserves under the Indian Act confined Indigenous peoples to small, often unsuitable parcels of land, effectively stifling their economic potential and cultural practices.

Contemporary Challenges in Land Reclamation

Systemic Barriers: Modern-day challenges in land reclamation are deeply rooted in the legacy of colonialism and the ongoing control exercised by federal and provincial governments. Despite numerous legal victories and modern treaties, Indigenous communities frequently face bureaucratic hurdles, slow implementation of agreements, and limited access to resources necessary for effective land management.

Legal and Political Struggles: The struggle for land rights continues through legal battles and political advocacy. Landmark cases like those of the Tsilhqot'in Nation, Innu Nation, and Ktunaxa Nation have affirmed Indigenous land rights, but the path to full recognition and implementation remains fraught with challenges. Indigenous communities often face protracted legal processes and resistance from various stakeholders, including government and industry actors.

Economic and Social Impacts: The historical and ongoing land dispossession has profound economic and social impacts on Indigenous communities. Limited land and resource access constrains economic development opportunities and perpetuates socio-economic disparities. The reserve system, with its constrained land holdings and lack of control over resources, exacerbates issues such as poverty, inadequate infrastructure, and dependency on government assistance.

Cultural Disintegration: The disruption of traditional land use practices and the forced relocation of Indigenous communities have had lasting effects on cultural continuity. The disconnection from ancestral lands has undermined traditional governance systems, cultural practices, and community cohesion. Efforts to reclaim land are not only about economic benefits but also about restoring cultural identity and autonomy.

Modern Reconciliation Efforts: Despite advancements in reconciliation and land claims agreements, the implementation of these agreements often falls short of expectations. Modern treaties, such as the Nunavut Land Claims Agreement, have made significant strides in recognizing Indigenous rights and providing resource revenue-sharing opportunities. However, the full realization of these agreements requires ongoing commitment, resources, and collaboration between governments and Indigenous communities.

The Importance of Continued Advocacy and Action to Address Indigenous Land Issues

The journey toward rectifying the historical and ongoing injustices faced by Indigenous communities in Canada is far from over. While there have been notable achievements in the realm of land rights and reconciliation, the road ahead demands sustained advocacy and concerted action. This section underscores why continued efforts are crucial for addressing these issues and advancing justice for Indigenous peoples.

Why Advocacy Matters

1. Addressing Historical Injustices: The dispossession of Indigenous lands and the erosion of cultural practices have deep historical roots. Advocacy plays a vital role in keeping these issues in the public eye, ensuring that the historical injustices are acknowledged and addressed. By maintaining pressure on government bodies and institutions, advocates help prevent the erasure of Indigenous histories and push for rectification measures that honor past agreements and rectify wrongs.

2. Influencing Policy and Legislation: Effective advocacy is instrumental in shaping public policy and legislative frameworks. Indigenous advocates and allies have been pivotal in challenging and reforming poli-

cies that perpetuate inequities. Continued advocacy is necessary to ensure that new policies and laws are crafted with genuine respect for Indigenous rights and interests, and that existing ones are enforced or amended to reflect contemporary realities.

3. Raising Public Awareness: Public awareness is a crucial component of advocacy. Many Canadians are unaware of the depth of the issues surrounding Indigenous land rights and the ongoing impacts of historical injustices. Advocacy efforts that focus on education and awareness help bridge the knowledge gap, fostering a more informed and empathetic public. This awareness can translate into increased support for policy changes and more substantial efforts toward reconciliation.

4. Empowering Indigenous Voices: Continued advocacy amplifies Indigenous voices and perspectives, ensuring that they are central to discussions and decision-making processes about land and resources. Indigenous leadership and grassroots organizations are at the forefront of these efforts, advocating for their communities' needs and aspirations. Supporting these voices empowers Indigenous peoples to lead the conversation about their future and ensures that their rights and priorities are recognized.

5. Ensuring Implementation and Accountability: Even when legal victories and agreements are achieved, implementation can be slow and fraught with challenges. Advocacy is crucial in holding governments and institutions accountable for fulfilling their commitments. By monitoring the progress of agreements, ensuring transparency, and demanding accountability, advocates help to ensure that promises are kept and that the benefits of agreements are realized by the communities they are meant to serve.

Action Steps for Continued Advocacy

1. Strengthening Alliances: Building strong alliances between Indigenous communities, advocacy groups, and sympathetic allies is essential. Collaborative efforts can amplify the impact of advocacy campaigns

and foster a unified voice in pushing for change. These alliances can also provide critical support in navigating legal and political challenges.

2. Engaging in Legal and Political Processes: Active participation in legal and political processes is a key strategy for advocacy. This includes pursuing litigation when necessary, engaging with policymakers, and participating in consultations and negotiations. Advocacy efforts should focus on both challenging harmful policies and supporting initiatives that advance Indigenous rights.

3. Promoting Education and Awareness: Educational campaigns and awareness-raising activities are vital for fostering public support and understanding. Advocates should continue to work on informing the public about Indigenous land issues, the significance of reconciliation, and the need for justice. This can be achieved through media, community events, and educational programs.

4. Supporting Indigenous-led Initiatives: Supporting Indigenous-led initiatives and organizations is crucial for empowering communities and driving change. This includes providing financial resources, technical assistance, and advocacy support for Indigenous-led land reclamation efforts, cultural revitalization projects, and self-governance initiatives.

5. Monitoring and Reporting: Ongoing monitoring and reporting on the state of Indigenous land rights and the implementation of agreements help maintain accountability and transparency. Advocacy groups should continue to assess the impact of policies, report on progress, and highlight areas where further action is needed.

6. Encouraging Policy Reform: Advocates should work to influence policy reform at both the federal and provincial levels. This includes advocating for laws and regulations that support Indigenous land rights, promote equitable resource management, and address systemic barriers to land reclamation.

The Future of Indigenous Land Rights in Canada

Looking Ahead: Toward a More Just and Sustainable Relationship Between Indigenous Peoples and Their Lands

Introduction: The Historical Context

The relationship between Indigenous peoples and their lands is both profound and complex, rooted in centuries of stewardship, cultural practices, and spiritual beliefs. For Indigenous communities, the land is not merely a resource to be exploited but a living entity that sustains life, culture, and identity. However, this relationship has been severely disrupted by colonialism, land dispossession, and environmental degradation. As we look ahead to the possibilities for a more just and sustainable relationship between Indigenous peoples and their lands, it is crucial to understand the historical context that has shaped these dynamics.

Colonial practices systematically stripped Indigenous communities of their lands, often through violent means, leading to widespread displacement and the erosion of traditional ways of life. The imposition of Western legal frameworks further alienated Indigenous peoples from their ancestral territories, prioritizing land ownership models that were incompatible with Indigenous worldviews. This history of dispossession is not just a relic of the past; its impacts are still felt today, manifesting in ongoing legal battles, environmental injustices, and socio-economic disparities.

Acknowledging and Redressing Historical Injustices

One of the first steps toward fostering a more just relationship between Indigenous peoples and their lands is to acknowledge and redress these historical injustices. This involves not only recognizing the wrongs of the past but also taking concrete actions to restore land rights and sovereignty to Indigenous communities. In recent years, there has been a growing movement toward land restitution and the recognition of Indigenous land rights, with some governments and institutions beginning to return lands to Indigenous peoples or provide compensation for past wrongs.

However, these efforts must go beyond mere tokenism. Genuine reconciliation requires meaningful dialogue with Indigenous communities, ensuring that they have a voice in decisions affecting their lands. This includes respecting Indigenous governance structures and traditional ecological knowledge, which have been honed over millennia and offer valuable insights into sustainable land management. By integrating Indigenous perspectives into land management practices, we can begin to repair the damage caused by colonialism and move toward a more equitable future.

The Role of Indigenous Knowledge in Sustainable Land Management

Indigenous knowledge systems, often referred to as Traditional Ecological Knowledge (TEK), are holistic and encompass a deep understanding of the interconnections between land, water, plants, animals, and people. Unlike Western approaches to land management, which often prioritize short-term economic gains, TEK emphasizes sustainability, reciprocity, and the well-being of all living beings. This knowledge is crucial for addressing the environmental challenges we face today, such as climate change, biodiversity loss, and ecosystem degradation.

Incorporating Indigenous knowledge into contemporary land management practices offers a pathway to sustainability that aligns with the principles of environmental stewardship and social justice. For example, traditional fire management techniques, such as controlled burning, have been shown to reduce the risk of catastrophic wildfires while promoting the health of ecosystems. Similarly, Indigenous practices of agroforestry and sustainable harvesting can enhance biodiversity and ensure the long-term productivity of the land.

However, the integration of Indigenous knowledge into mainstream practices must be done with respect and recognition of its cultural significance. This means that Indigenous peoples should lead these initiatives, with their knowledge and expertise valued and compensated appropriately. Collaborative partnerships between Indigenous communities, governments, and environmental organizations can help bridge the gap between traditional and modern practices, fostering a more sustainable and just relationship with the land.

Legal and Policy Frameworks Supporting Indigenous Land Rights

The recognition of Indigenous land rights is increasingly being reflected in legal and policy frameworks around the world. International instruments such as the United Nations Declaration on the Rights of Indigenous Peoples (UNDRIP) provide a foundation for the protection and promotion of Indigenous land rights, including the right to free, prior, and informed consent (FPIC) regarding land and resource decisions. Additionally, some countries have begun to enshrine Indigenous land rights in their constitutions or national legislation, providing legal avenues for the restitution of lands and the protection of Indigenous territories from exploitation.

Despite these advancements, significant challenges remain. Many Indigenous communities continue to face legal barriers in asserting their land rights, particularly in regions where land tenure systems are complex or where governments are resistant to recognizing Indigenous sovereignty. Moreover, the enforcement of existing legal protections is often inconsistent, with Indigenous lands frequently subjected to illegal logging, mining, and other forms of exploitation.

To overcome these challenges, there is a need for stronger legal protections and greater political will to uphold Indigenous land rights. This includes ensuring that legal frameworks are aligned with Indigenous worldviews and governance structures, rather than imposing external models that may not be compatible with Indigenous ways of life. Furthermore, the legal recognition of Indigenous land rights should be accompanied by the necessary resources and support to enable Indigenous communities to effectively manage and protect their lands.

The Future: Building Alliances for a Just and Sustainable Relationship

As we look to the future, building alliances between Indigenous peoples, environmental advocates, policymakers, and broader society will be essential in creating a more just and sustainable relationship with the land. These alliances should be grounded in mutual respect, with an em-

phasis on shared goals such as environmental conservation, climate justice, and the protection of Indigenous cultures and ways of life.

One promising avenue for collaboration is the growing movement
for Indigenous-led conservation. Across the globe, Indigenous communities are establishing protected areas and conservation initiatives that
prioritize both ecological integrity and cultural preservation. These initiatives often challenge conventional conservation models, which have
historically excluded Indigenous peoples, instead offering a more inclusive and holistic approach to environmental stewardship.

In addition to conservation efforts, there is a need for broader societal shifts in how we understand and relate to the land. This includes
challenging the dominant narratives of land as a commodity and instead
embracing Indigenous perspectives that see the land as a living entity de-
serving of respect and care. Education and awareness-raising efforts can
play a crucial role in this, helping to foster a deeper appreciation for Indigenous knowledge and the importance of land sovereignty.

Finally, the pursuit of a just and sustainable relationship with Indigenous peoples and their lands must be an ongoing process, one that is
responsive to the evolving needs and aspirations of Indigenous communities. This requires continuous engagement, the willingness to listen
and learn, and a commitment to supporting Indigenous-led initiatives
that advance both social justice and environmental sustainability.

The Role of All Canadians in Supporting Indigenous Land Rights
and Contributing to a More Inclusive Society

Introduction: A Shared Responsibility

Canada's history is deeply intertwined with the experiences and
struggles of its Indigenous peoples. For centuries, Indigenous communities have faced systemic marginalization, cultural erasure, and the dispossession of their lands. While these injustices are rooted in the past,
their effects are still very much present, influencing the lives of Indigenous peoples today. As Canadians, we all have a role to play in addressing these historical wrongs and contributing to a more inclusive and

equitable society. This responsibility extends beyond mere acknowledgment; it calls for active participation in supporting Indigenous land rights and fostering a society where Indigenous cultures and identities are respected and celebrated.

The path toward reconciliation is not solely the burden of Indigenous peoples; it is a collective journey that requires the involvement of all Canadians. By understanding the importance of Indigenous land rights, advocating for justice, and embracing cultural diversity, Canadians can contribute to a future that honors the sovereignty and dignity of Indigenous communities.

Understanding the Importance of Indigenous Land Rights

Land is central to the identity, culture, and well-being of Indigenous peoples. It is the foundation upon which their societies are built, providing not only sustenance but also spiritual and cultural connections that are integral to their way of life. The dispossession of Indigenous lands through colonization has had devastating consequences, leading to the loss of traditional livelihoods, the erosion of cultural practices, and the displacement of communities.

Supporting Indigenous land rights is not just about returning physical territories; it is about recognizing and respecting the profound relationship that Indigenous peoples have with their lands. This recognition is crucial for the preservation of Indigenous cultures and the promotion of environmental stewardship. When Indigenous communities have control over their lands, they can continue to practice sustainable land management and pass down their knowledge to future generations.

For Canadians, understanding the importance of Indigenous land rights begins with education. Learning about the history of land dispossession, the legal struggles for land restitution, and the ongoing efforts to protect Indigenous territories is essential. This knowledge empowers Canadians to become informed advocates for Indigenous land rights and to support policies and initiatives that prioritize the sovereignty of Indigenous peoples over their lands.

Advocacy and Allyship: Moving Beyond Words

Advocating for Indigenous land rights involves more than just vocal support; it requires concrete actions that contribute to meaningful change. Canadians can play an active role in this advocacy by supporting Indigenous-led movements, engaging with local Indigenous organizations, and amplifying the voices of Indigenous leaders and activists.

One way to demonstrate allyship is by participating in campaigns and initiatives that seek to protect Indigenous lands from exploitation. This could involve supporting legal battles against resource extraction projects that threaten Indigenous territories, advocating for the implementation of the United Nations Declaration on the Rights of Indigenous Peoples (UNDRIP), or joining efforts to secure land restitution for displaced communities.

Furthermore, Canadians can use their positions of influence, whether in the workplace, educational institutions, or community organizations, to push for policies and practices that respect Indigenous land rights. This might include promoting ethical investment practices that do not contribute to the exploitation of Indigenous lands, advocating for the inclusion of Indigenous perspectives in decision-making processes, or supporting initiatives that seek to preserve and revitalize Indigenous languages and cultures.

Allyship also means being accountable and willing to listen. It involves recognizing the power dynamics that have historically silenced Indigenous voices and actively working to ensure that these voices are heard and respected. By standing in solidarity with Indigenous communities, Canadians can help to create a more just and equitable society where Indigenous rights are not only recognized but upheld.

Embracing Cultural Diversity and Inclusion

A more inclusive society is one that values and celebrates the cultural diversity that Indigenous peoples bring to the fabric of Canada. Indigenous cultures, languages, and traditions are not relics of the past; they are vibrant and dynamic, contributing to the richness of Canadian society. However, for far too long, Indigenous cultures have been marginalized, and their contributions have been overlooked.

To foster a truly inclusive society, Canadians must actively engage with Indigenous cultures in ways that are respectful and informed. This means seeking out opportunities to learn from Indigenous knowledge holders, participating in cultural events and ceremonies with an open heart, and supporting the work of Indigenous artists, writers, and creators. By doing so, Canadians can help to ensure that Indigenous cultures are not only preserved but also celebrated as an integral part of the nation's identity.

Education plays a critical role in this process. Schools, universities, and other educational institutions must prioritize the inclusion of Indigenous histories, cultures, and perspectives in their curricula. This is not only about teaching the historical facts of colonization and its impacts but also about fostering an appreciation for the resilience and contributions of Indigenous peoples. When Canadians are educated about Indigenous cultures from a young age, they are more likely to grow into adults who value diversity and advocate for inclusion.

Moreover, inclusion must extend beyond cultural appreciation to address the systemic inequalities that continue to affect Indigenous communities. This includes tackling issues such as poverty, inadequate access to healthcare and education, and the overrepresentation of Indigenous peoples in the criminal justice system. By addressing these disparities, Canadians can contribute to a society where all individuals, regardless of their background, have the opportunity to thrive.

Building Relationships Based on Mutual Respect

At the heart of supporting Indigenous land rights and fostering an inclusive society is the need to build relationships based on mutual respect. Reconciliation is not a one-time event or a box to be checked; it is an ongoing process that requires continuous effort and commitment. This process involves listening to Indigenous voices, acknowledging past wrongs, and working together to create a future that reflects the values of equity, justice, and respect.

For Canadians, building these relationships starts with humility and a willingness to learn. It means approaching conversations with Indigenous peoples with an open mind and a genuine desire to understand their experiences and perspectives. It also means being aware of one's own biases and privileges, and how these may affect interactions with Indigenous communities.

Building respectful relationships also involves supporting the self-determination of Indigenous peoples. This means recognizing their right to make decisions about their lands, cultures, and futures without external interference. Canadians can support self-determination by advocating for policies that empower Indigenous communities, such as those that promote Indigenous-led education, healthcare, and economic development.

Ultimately, building relationships based on mutual respect requires a commitment to walking alongside Indigenous peoples on the path to reconciliation. It means standing in solidarity with their struggles, celebrating their successes, and working together to create a society that honors the contributions and rights of all its members.

The End

9

Appendices

K ey Legal Documents and Treaties
Introduction: The Legal Foundation of Indigenous Land
Rights

The legal recognition of Indigenous land rights in Canada has been shaped by a complex history of treaties, legal texts, and agreements that continue to influence the relationship between Indigenous peoples and the Canadian state. These documents form the foundation of Indigenous claims to land, sovereignty, and self-determination. They are not merely historical artifacts but living instruments that continue to guide contemporary legal and political discussions around Indigenous rights.

Understanding the significance of these legal texts and agreements is essential for anyone interested in Indigenous land rights. They provide critical insights into the commitments made by both Indigenous peoples and the Crown, the evolution of legal frameworks, and the ongoing struggle for recognition and implementation of these rights. This section reproduces and discusses some of the most important legal documents, treaties, and agreements that are central to Indigenous land rights in Canada.

The Royal Proclamation of 1763

One of the earliest and most significant legal texts related to Indigenous land rights in Canada is the Royal Proclamation of 1763. Issued by King George III, the Proclamation established British administrative control over territories in North America following the Seven Years' War. Importantly, it recognized Indigenous peoples' rights to their lands and established a legal framework for treaty-making between the Crown and Indigenous nations.

The Royal Proclamation is often cited as a foundational document in Canadian constitutional law, particularly in relation to Indigenous land rights. It asserted that Indigenous lands could not be taken or purchased by private individuals, and that only the Crown could negotiate land cessions through treaties with Indigenous nations. This recognition of Indigenous land rights was groundbreaking at the time and continues to be referenced in legal arguments and court decisions concerning Indigenous sovereignty.

Excerpts from the Royal Proclamation of 1763:

"... And whereas it is just and reasonable, and essential to our Interest and the Security of our Colonies, that the several Nations or Tribes of Indians with whom We are connected, and who live under our Protection, should not be molested or disturbed in the Possession of such Parts of Our Dominions and Territories as, not having been ceded to or purchased by Us, are reserved to them, or any of them, as their Hunting Grounds."

"... We do therefore, with the Advice of our Privy Council, declare it to be our Royal Will and Pleasure, that no Governor or Commander in Chief in any of our Colonies of Quebec, East Florida, or West Florida, do presume, upon any Pretence whatever, to grant Warrants of Survey, or pass any Patents for Lands beyond the Bounds of their respective Governments, as described in their Commissions; as also that no Governor or Commander in Chief of our other Colonies or Plantations in America do presume for the present, and until Our further Pleasure be known, to grant Warrants of Survey, or pass Patents for any Lands beyond the Heads or Sources of any of the Rivers which fall into the Atlantic Ocean from the West or Northwest, or upon any Lands whatever, which, not having been ceded to or purchased by Us as aforesaid, are reserved to the said Indians, or any of them."

The Royal Proclamation of 1763 laid the groundwork for future treaties and has been cited in numerous legal cases as a basis for Indigenous land rights.

Numbered Treaties (1871–1921)

The Numbered Treaties, a series of eleven treaties signed between Indigenous peoples and the Canadian government between 1871 and 1921, were pivotal in the expansion of Canadian settlement across the prairies and into the northern territories. These treaties involved the cession of vast tracts of Indigenous lands to the Crown in exchange for various promises, including the provision of reserves, annuities, education, and farming tools. However, the interpretation and implementation of these treaties have been contentious, with many Indigenous communities arguing that the Canadian government has failed to uphold the promises made.

The text of the Numbered Treaties typically included provisions for land cession, the establishment of reserves, and the protection of hunting, fishing, and trapping rights. However, there were significant differences in the understanding of these treaties between the Indigenous signatories and the Crown, leading to ongoing disputes and legal challenges.

Excerpts from Treaty No. 6 (1876):

"The Plain and Wood Cree Tribes of Indians, and all other the Indians inhabiting the district hereinafter described and defined, do hereby cede, release, surrender and yield up to the Government of the Dominion of Canada, for Her Majesty the Queen and her successors forever, all their rights, titles and privileges whatsoever, to the lands included within the following limits, that is to say: [detailed description of the lands]."

"And Her Majesty the Queen hereby agrees and undertakes to lay aside reserves for farming lands for the Indians, such lands to be selected by officers of Her Majesty's Government, and the Government of Canada further agrees to maintain schools for instruction in such reserves hereby made."

The Numbered Treaties remain a source of significant legal and political debate. Many Indigenous communities assert that these treaties were intended to establish a relationship of partnership and coexistence, rather than simply the transfer of land.

The Constitution Act, 1982 (Section 35)

The inclusion of Section 35 in the Constitution Act, 1982, marked a significant milestone in the recognition of Indigenous rights in Canada. Section 35 affirms and recognizes the existing Aboriginal and treaty rights of the Indigenous peoples of Canada. This constitutional recognition has provided a powerful legal tool for Indigenous communities to assert their rights in courts and has led to numerous landmark legal decisions that have clarified and expanded the scope of these rights.

Section 35 does not define the specific rights it protects, which has led to extensive litigation to determine the nature and extent of these rights. Courts have interpreted Section 35 to include not only rights explicitly outlined in treaties but also those arising from Indigenous customs, practices, and traditions.

Text of Section 35, Constitution Act, 1982:

"35. (1) The existing aboriginal and treaty rights of the aboriginal peoples of Canada are hereby recognized and affirmed.

(2) In this Act, 'aboriginal peoples of Canada' includes the Indian, Inuit, and Métis peoples of Canada.

(3) For greater certainty, in subsection (1) 'treaty rights' includes rights that now exist by way of land claims agreements or may be so acquired.

(4) Notwithstanding any other provision of this Act, the aboriginal and treaty rights referred to in subsection (1) are guaranteed equally to male and female persons."

Section 35 has been instrumental in advancing Indigenous land rights, leading to significant legal victories for Indigenous communities, including the recognition of title, hunting and fishing rights, and the duty of the Crown to consult and accommodate Indigenous peoples in decisions affecting their lands.

The United Nations Declaration on the Rights of Indigenous Peoples (UNDRIP)

The United Nations Declaration on the Rights of Indigenous Peoples (UNDRIP), adopted by the United Nations General Assembly in 2007, is a comprehensive international instrument that sets out the rights of Indigenous peoples, including their rights to land, territories, and resources. While not legally binding, UNDRIP has been widely recognized as an important standard for the treatment of Indigenous peoples and has influenced legal and policy reforms in many countries, including Canada.

In 2016, Canada officially adopted UNDRIP, committing to its full implementation in Canadian law and policy. This commitment was further solidified with the passage of Bill C-15, the United Nations Declaration on the Rights of Indigenous Peoples Act, in 2021, which requires the federal government to align Canadian laws with UNDRIP and to develop a national action plan to achieve its objectives.

Excerpts from UNDRIP:

"Article 26

Indigenous peoples have the right to the lands, territories and resources which they have traditionally owned, occupied or otherwise used or acquired.

Indigenous peoples have the right to own, use, develop and control the lands, territories and resources that they possess by reason of traditional ownership or other traditional occupation or use, as well as those which they have otherwise acquired.

States shall give legal recognition and protection to these lands, territories and resources. Such recognition shall be conducted with due respect to the customs, traditions and land tenure systems of the Indigenous peoples concerned."

UNDRIP represents a global consensus on the rights of Indigenous peoples and provides a framework for advancing Indigenous land rights in Canada. The ongoing challenge is to translate the principles of UN-

DRIP into tangible legal and policy outcomes that respect and uphold Indigenous sovereignty.

List of Key Indigenous Organizations and Resources

Introduction: The Importance of Advocacy and Support

Supporting Indigenous land rights is a crucial aspect of fostering a just and equitable society. Across Canada, numerous organizations are dedicated to advocating for the rights of Indigenous peoples, providing legal support, and working to ensure that Indigenous communities have the resources and recognition needed to protect their lands and cultures. These organizations play a vital role in the ongoing struggle for land rights, offering legal assistance, raising awareness, and facilitating community-led initiatives.

Below is a list of key organizations involved in land rights advocacy and support for Indigenous communities in Canada. This list includes contact information, descriptions of their work, and the specific areas they focus on.

1. Assembly of First Nations (AFN)

Description: The Assembly of First Nations (AFN) is a national advocacy organization representing First Nations across Canada. The AFN works to advance the rights and interests of First Nations, including land rights, self-determination, and governance. The organization engages with the federal government, international bodies, and other stakeholders to advocate for the recognition and implementation of treaty rights, land claims, and other critical issues affecting First Nations.

Key Areas of Focus:

Land and resource rights

Treaty implementation

Self-governance and sovereignty

Environmental protection

Contact Information:

Website: www.afn.ca
Phone: +1 (613) 241-6789
Email: info@afn.ca
Address: 55 Metcalfe Street, Suite 1600, Ottawa, ON K1P 6L5, Canada
    2. Indigenous Land Stewardship Circle (ILSC)
    Description: The Indigenous Land Stewardship Circle (ILSC) is a coalition of Indigenous leaders, environmental organizations, and allies dedicated to promoting Indigenous-led land stewardship practices. The ILSC supports Indigenous communities in protecting their lands and resources, promoting sustainable land management, and advancing Indigenous rights within environmental conservation efforts.
    Key Areas of Focus:
    Indigenous land stewardship
Environmental conservation
Advocacy for Indigenous rights in environmental policies
Community-led land management initiatives
    Contact Information:
    Website: www.ilscircle.org
Email: contact@ilscircle.org
Address: (Please visit their website for specific contact details and regional offices)
    3. Canadian Association of Elizabeth Fry Societies (CAEFS)
    Description: While primarily focused on social justice and advocacy for women in the criminal justice system, the Canadian Association of Elizabeth Fry Societies (CAEFS) also engages in advocacy related to Indigenous rights, particularly concerning the overrepresentation of Indigenous women in the criminal justice system and the intersection with land rights and sovereignty issues. CAEFS works to address the broader socio-economic factors that contribute to the marginalization of Indigenous communities, including land dispossession.
    Key Areas of Focus:

Advocacy for Indigenous women

Social justice and criminal justice reform

Intersection of land rights and socio-economic issues

Contact Information:

Website: www.caefs.ca

Phone: +1 (613) 238-2422

Email: caefs@caefs.ca

Address: 701-151 Slater Street, Ottawa, ON K1P 5H3, Canada

4. First Peoples Law

Description: First Peoples Law is a law firm dedicated to defending and advancing the rights of Indigenous peoples across Canada. The firm provides legal services to Indigenous communities, focusing on land rights, governance, and consultation processes. First Peoples Law also engages in public education and advocacy to raise awareness about Indigenous rights and legal issues.

Key Areas of Focus:

Legal representation for Indigenous communities

Land claims and title cases

Consultation and accommodation processes

Public education on Indigenous rights

Contact Information:

Website: www.firstpeopleslaw.com

Phone: +1 (604) 685-4240

Email: info@firstpeopleslaw.com

Address: Suite 209, 100 Park Royal, West Vancouver, BC V7T 1A2, Canada

5. Land Claims Agreements Coalition (LCAC)

Description: The Land Claims Agreements Coalition (LCAC) is an organization that represents Indigenous groups in Canada with modern land claims agreements. The coalition works to ensure that these agreements are fully implemented and respected by the federal and provincial governments. The LCAC advocates for policy changes, educates the public about the importance of land claims, and supports member communities in their efforts to secure and manage their lands.

Key Areas of Focus:

Implementation of modern land claims agreements

Policy advocacy and reform

Education and public awareness

Support for member communities

Contact Information:

Website: www.landclaimscoalition.ça

Phone: +1 (613) 236-9460

Email: info@landclaimscoalition.ca

Address: 75 Albert Street, Suite 1200, Ottawa, ON K1P 5E7, Canada

6. The Indigenous Bar Association (IBA)

Description: The Indigenous Bar Association (IBA) is a non-profit organization representing Indigenous lawyers, judges, law students, and legal scholars in Canada. The IBA advocates for the recognition and advancement of Indigenous legal traditions and supports the development of laws and policies that uphold Indigenous land rights and sovereignty. The association also provides a platform for Indigenous legal professionals to collaborate and share knowledge.

Key Areas of Focus:

Advocacy for Indigenous legal traditions

Support for Indigenous legal professionals

Policy development on land rights and sovereignty

Public education on Indigenous law

Contact Information:

Website: www.indigenousbar.ca

Email: admin@indigenousbar.ca

Address: 3rd Floor, 75 Albert Street, Ottawa, ON K1P 5E7, Canada

7. Union of British Columbia Indian Chiefs (UBCIC)

Description: The Union of British Columbia Indian Chiefs (UBCIC) is an Indigenous political organization that advocates for the recognition and protection of Indigenous title and rights in British Columbia. The UBCIC works to advance Indigenous land rights, challenge unjust policies, and support self-determination for Indigenous communities in the province. The organization is deeply involved in legal advocacy, public education, and policy development.

Key Areas of Focus:

Indigenous title and rights

Legal and policy advocacy

Self-determination and governance

Public education on Indigenous issues

Contact Information:

Website: www.ubcic.bc.ca

Phone: +1 (604) 684-0231

Email: info@ubcic.bc.ca

Address: 312 Main Street, Suite 401, Vancouver, BC V6A 2T2, Canada

Conclusion: Supporting the Work for Justice

These organizations play a critical role in the ongoing struggle for Indigenous land rights in Canada. By supporting their work, Canadians can contribute to efforts that seek justice, recognition, and respect for Indigenous peoples and their lands. Whether through advocacy, legal assistance, education, or direct support to Indigenous communities, these organizations provide essential resources and guidance in the pursuit of a more equitable and inclusive society.

Canadians are encouraged to connect with these organizations, learn more about their work, and find ways to contribute to the collective effort to uphold Indigenous land rights and support Indigenous sovereignty.

Glossary of Terms

Definitions of Key Terms and Concepts Related to Indigenous Land Rights and Canadian Law

Introduction: The Language of Indigenous Land Rights

Understanding Indigenous land rights in Canada requires familiarity with a range of key terms and concepts that are central to discussions in law, policy, and advocacy. These terms often have specific meanings within the context of Indigenous rights and Canadian legal frameworks. Below is a glossary of important terms and concepts that are frequently encountered in discussions about Indigenous land rights.

1. Aboriginal Rights

Definition: Aboriginal rights are collective rights that stem from the original occupancy of land by Indigenous peoples in Canada before European colonization. These rights are inherent and not granted by the state, including rights to land, resources, and cultural practices. Aboriginal rights are recognized and affirmed under Section 35 of the Constitution Act, 1982.

Example: Aboriginal rights can include the right to hunt, fish, and gather on ancestral lands, as well as the right to practice traditional ceremonies.

2. Treaty Rights

Definition: Treaty rights are specific rights that Indigenous peoples hold as a result of treaties negotiated and signed between Indigenous nations and the Crown. These rights vary depending on the terms of the treaty but often include provisions for land, hunting, fishing, and self-governance.

Example: The Numbered Treaties, signed between 1871 and 1921, include treaty rights to reserves, annuities, and the protection of hunting and fishing practices.

3. Indigenous Title (or Aboriginal Title)

Definition: Indigenous title, also known as Aboriginal title, is a legal concept that recognizes Indigenous peoples' inherent rights to their ancestral lands. It is based on the longstanding use and occupation of the land by Indigenous communities before European colonization. Indigenous title is distinct from other forms of land ownership recognized by Canadian law.

Example: In the landmark case Delgamuukw v. British Columbia (1997), the Supreme Court of Canada recognized the existence of Aboriginal title and set out the test for proving such title.

4. The Duty to Consult and Accommodate

Definition: The duty to consult and accommodate is a legal obligation that requires the Crown to engage with Indigenous peoples when considering actions or decisions that may affect their rights, particularly land and resource rights. This duty arises from Section 35 of the Constitution Act, 1982, and aims to protect Indigenous interests by ensuring that their voices are heard in decisions impacting their lands.

Example: The duty to consult and accommodate was highlighted in the Haida Nation v. British Columbia (Minister of Forests) (2004) case, where the Supreme Court of Canada ruled that the Crown must consult with the Haida Nation before making decisions that could affect their land rights.

5. Free, Prior, and Informed Consent (FPIC)

Definition: Free, Prior, and Informed Consent (FPIC) is a principle that recognizes the right of Indigenous peoples to give or withhold consent to projects that may affect their lands, territories, and resources. FPIC is a key component of the United Nations Declaration on the Rights of Indigenous Peoples (UNDRIP) and is intended to protect Indigenous sovereignty and self-determination.

Example: FPIC requires that Indigenous communities are fully informed about the potential impacts of a proposed development project on their lands and are given the opportunity to consent or reject the project before it proceeds.

6. Reserves

Definition: Reserves are parcels of land set aside by the Crown for the use and benefit of Indigenous communities. Reserves were often established through treaties or by government action. While Indigenous communities have the right to live on and use reserve lands, the ultimate legal title to the land is held by the Crown.

Example: The creation of reserves was a common feature of the Numbered Treaties, where the Crown promised to provide designated lands for Indigenous communities in exchange for the cession of larger territories.

7. Sovereignty

Definition: Sovereignty refers to the inherent authority of Indigenous nations to govern themselves, make decisions about their lands, resources, and people, and exercise their cultural and political rights without external interference. Indigenous sovereignty is often asserted in contrast to the sovereignty claimed by the Canadian state.

Example: Many Indigenous nations in Canada assert their sovereignty through the establishment of traditional governance systems and the pursuit of self-determination initiatives.

8. The Constitution Act, 1982 (Section 35)

Definition: Section 35 of the Constitution Act, 1982, is a key legal provision that recognizes and affirms the existing Aboriginal and treaty rights of Indigenous peoples in Canada. It provides constitutional protection for these rights and has been the foundation for many significant legal cases involving Indigenous land claims and rights.

Example: Section 35 has been central to legal cases such as R. v. Sparrow (1990), where the Supreme Court of Canada affirmed the existence of Aboriginal rights to fish and established a test for determining when these rights can be justifiably infringed.

9. Modern Treaties (Comprehensive Land Claims Agreements)

Definition: Modern treaties, also known as Comprehensive Land Claims Agreements, are agreements negotiated between Indigenous groups, the federal government, and provincial or territorial governments to resolve outstanding land claims. These treaties address land ownership, resource rights, self-governance, and financial compensation, among other issues.

Example: The Nunavut Land Claims Agreement, signed in 1993, is a modern treaty that led to the creation of the territory of Nunavut and provided Inuit with land ownership, resource rights, and self-government powers.

10. Self-Governance

Definition: Self-governance refers to the right and ability of Indigenous communities to govern themselves, make decisions about their internal affairs, and exercise control over their lands and resources. Self-governance is a key aspect of Indigenous sovereignty and is often negotiated as part of modern treaties and land claims agreements.

Example: The Nisga'a Final Agreement, signed in 1998, includes provisions for self-governance, allowing the Nisga'a Nation to manage its own government, laws, and land-use planning.

11. Land Restitution

Definition: Land restitution involves the return of lands to Indigenous peoples that were taken from them through colonization, treaties, or other means. It is a form of reparation aimed at addressing historical injustices and restoring Indigenous peoples' connection to their ancestral territories.

Example: In recent years, there have been instances where governments have returned lands to Indigenous communities as part of settlement agreements or reconciliation initiatives.

12. The Royal Proclamation of 1763

Definition: The Royal Proclamation of 1763 is a historic document issued by King George III that recognized Indigenous peoples' rights to their lands and established a framework for the negotiation of treaties. It is considered a foundational document in Canadian law regarding Indigenous land rights.

Example: The Royal Proclamation is often cited in legal cases as evidence of the Crown's recognition of Indigenous land rights and the requirement for treaties to cede land.

13. Land Claims

Definition: Land claims refer to legal assertions made by Indigenous peoples seeking recognition of their rights to lands that were taken from them or that were never ceded through treaties. Land claims can be specific, relating to a particular area of land, or comprehensive, addressing broader territorial claims.

Example: The Tsilhqot'in Nation v. British Columbia (2014) case involved a comprehensive land claim, where the Supreme Court of

Canada recognized the Tsilhqot'in Nation's Aboriginal title to a large area of land in British Columbia.

Printed in the USA
CPSIA information can be obtained
at www.ICGtesting.com
CBHW071500261024
16328CB00047BA/757